A Cross Stitcher's
ORIENTAL ODYSSEY

A Cross Stitcher's
ORIENTAL
ODYSSEY

JOAN ELLIOTT *for*
DESIGN WORKS CRAFTS

David & Charles

For my parents, Hedy and Howard

A DAVID & CHARLES BOOK

First published in the UK in 2001

Text and designs Copyright © Joan Elliott for Design Works Crafts Inc. 2001
Layout Copyright © David & Charles 2001

Photographs on pp 5, 21, 25, 43, 53, 58–9, 61, 64–5, 66, 68, 77, 88–9, 95, 105, 107, 108 by
    David & Kit Johnson Copyright © David & Charles 2001
Artworks on page 104 by Ethan Danielson Copyright © David & Charles 2001
Photography on pp 1, 2, 6, 7, 9, 11, 13, 14, 15, 20, 26, 28, 30, 32, 34–5, 36, 37, 47, 52, 70–1,
    83, 97 by Donna Richardson Copyright © Design Works Crafts 2001
Photographs on pp 1, 6, 7, 9, 13, 36, 37 from author's collection

Project editing and chart manipulation by Linda Clements

Printed in Italy by Milanostampa SpA
for David & Charles
Brunel House   Newton Abbot   Devon

*Page 1: 'Girl's Day' in Japan is on
3 March, celebrating their health
and beauty. Each year a new
hina-matsuri doll, representing
a member of the emperor's court, is
presented to the girls in the family.
In the picture on page 1 a lady-in-
waiting is dressed in the luxurious
layers of a colourful silk kimono*

Contents

Introduction

An odyssey is a series of adventures or journeys to places unknown and *A Cross Stitcher's Oriental Odyssey* will take you to a land where the threads of ancient art and cultural tradition are carefully woven together, bringing a sense of peace and harmony to our everyday environment. The sensuous colours of luxurious silk, the heady scent of spring flowers, the simple beauty of a flowing stream – all conjure up images of the Orient. This collection of designs brings those sensibilities to the art of cross stitch.

The projects I've created for this book have their roots in my own interest in Chinese and Japanese art. Creativity and everyday life come together beautifully in both cultures and the designs draw on several different aspects of that spirit. Reflected in the embroideries you will see the seduction of the kimono, the art of Japanese woodblock prints, the beauty of Chinese calligraphy, and the aesthetic discipline of feng shui. Nature, as an integral part of life, echoes through all the motifs.

Ukiyo-e woodblock prints were used in Edo Japan to depict scenes from everyday life. In this 1859 print by Kunisada, two women dressed in winter kimonos are out for a stroll with a playful child. (From Matching Pictures with the Chushingura – Act XII)

The Kimono – Fashion as Art

Nothing captures the essence of female beauty quite the way the kimono does. Billowing layers of painted and embroidered silk reflect centuries of culture and history. In twelfth century Japan, elite women spent much of their time wearing robes of twelve or more layers. In a subtle game of seduction, they were seated and concealed behind screens with only the slightest portion of the sleeves and hem of their garment visible. The colours for these costumes were carefully chosen to reflect the season, occasion; social class and each woman's personal feelings. This symbolic language mirrored her individuality and desirability. An aesthetic of hidden glamour was developed: beauty hinted at but not openly displayed.

Today the kimono is worn for special ceremonies and occasions but during the Edo period of Japan it was the ultimate symbol of affluence, to be worn and displayed whenever possible. It was here that the kimono became art as fashion. Spanning the seventeenth, eighteenth and the first half of the nineteenth centuries, Edo (named after the city we now know as Tokyo) Japan enjoyed a popularity of culture and creativity previously unknown. Improvements in education, agriculture and commerce gave rise to thriving urban centres, where sophisticated aesthetic sensibilities began to develop within the merchant and artisan classes. These were realms formerly reserved for the elite ruling classes. The growing prosperity increased the demand for more luxurious textiles and the kimono became the status symbol of the times. By the late seventeenth century, the expansion of wealth and culture significantly changed the textile industry. The woven silks patterned on the loom were now being embellished with embroidery, painting and tie-dye techniques.

The obi, a sash worn around the waist, also began to change. From its humble beginnings as a simple braided rope or flat sash, it developed into an elaborate accessory to the kimono. Intricate pattern and decoration adorned the obi and complex methods of tying them were fashioned to show them off to best advantage. As the trend towards more and more luxury continued, art and fashion began to merge. Textile design was approached as a true art form with the kimono as a huge blank canvas waiting for the artist's creation. The fervour of people to outdo each other in their dress reached such heights that the ruling shogun had to issue at least seven Sumptuary Laws in one year alone on the subject of dress. These laws sought to regulate the use of certain colours, materials and techniques. Underlying these restrictions was the desire to keep

Beautiful women were popular subjects for the artists of Edo Japan. The vibrant colours and graceful lines of this 1852 print by Kuniyoshi Utagawa create a lovely portrait. (From the Series Famous Products of the Province with Women's Postures – Kishu)

the class lines distinct, thus maintaining the status quo. As a result, people were continually inventing new ways to circumvent the laws, making their enforcement difficult.

In Edo Japan, a woman's clothing was her principal form of property. Kimono collections became heirlooms, with each generation carefully preserving the precious treasures. To see and be seen became the rule of the day. During day-long Kabuki theatre performances, attendees were known to change outfits several times, allowing them to openly display their wealth.

Painting – the Print and the Fan

The art of the Japanese print reached new heights during the Edo period. Artists created woodblock prints portraying actors, courtesans, the latest fashions and everyday street scenes, making these images available to everyone. The Ukiyo-e prints, literally pictures of the floating world, are the most often recognized. The rise of the merchant class created a demand for pictures of contemporary urban life. The floating world signified the transitory way of life that was so popular at the time, living for the moment and drifting with the trends. This idea culminated in the pleasure districts. It was here that the courtesans, skilled in music, poetry and the tea ceremony, reached lofty positions within their own social hierarchy. The most beautiful and intelligent women became ideal models for the print maker. Their swelling popularity made them the subject of the prose and theatre of the day.

The harmonious colours and sensuous lines used by the artists provided the Japanese urban middle class with a sense of artistic pleasure. This unique style also intrigued European artists of the time. By the latter half of the nineteenth century, Japan began to open its doors to the West. In 1872, the term Japonisme began to be used across Europe to describe

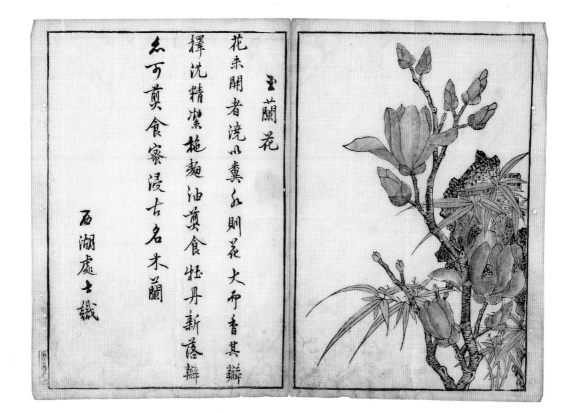

all things Japanese. Previously isolated from the rest of the world, Japan began to make its mark. The composition, colour and subject matter of the prints influenced artists such as Whistler, Manet and Degas. In fact, these sensibilities continued into the Art Nouveau period at the turn of the century. Alphonse Mucha, Gustav Klimt and Aubrey Beardsley are but a few of the artists who recognized the beauty of line and movement that the Japanese had mastered.

Dress, art, and culture in Edo Japan were completely interwoven. By the mid-nineteenth century, most of society was more urbane, literate and self-sufficient. Popular culture seemed to be all about flamboyance and affluence, but there was another movement underway at the same time. This was a trend defined by a more contemplative spirit, and included such arts as haiku poetry, ikebana flower arrangement and the tea ceremony. It is perhaps in

The early flower paintings of China reflect the artists' respect for nature. These pages of delicately rendered magnolias and the calligraphic text that describes them are from the sketchbook of Chinese naturalist, Hasshu Gaffu, and date from around 1710. (Magnolia Branch in Spring. From A Notebook on Flora and Fauna of China)

these disciplines that we can see the influence that China had on Japan.

Although considered isolated, Japan did import goods from China. Books and prints had a decisive impact on their artistic consciousness. The jewel-like colours and natural subjects of Chinese painting greatly inspired the nature prints of the Edo period. Both cultures produced exquisite hand-painted fans that became a respected art form. They played an important role, carried by both men and women. There were different classes of fans, each reserved for a special ceremony or use. Leading Chinese painters used the fan as a canvas for their finest work. Ethereal landscapes

Nature is a favourite subject of artists in every culture. Chinese artists expressed nature with particular grace and elegance. With careful attention to detail, they were able to capture the harmony and movement of the natural world

and vivid renditions of birds and flowers brought nature indoors. Painted with India ink and colour on paper or silk, fans were often finished with a sprinkling of gold dust or laid with gold or silver leaf. A poem or spiritual saying in calligraphy might complete the artwork.

Calligraphy – a Sacred Form

Without a writing method of their own, the Japanese adopted the Chinese script called kanji. Eventually, recognizing the need to write their own language, a new writing called kana developed. Like the Chinese, the Japanese eventually elevated their writing to a more aesthetic level. An artfully mastered piece of

calligraphy was the absolute expression of the writer's breeding, sensitivity and character.

Calligraphy is a sacred art form in China and it is said that the practice should take place only at moments of calm and tranquillity. This incomparably beautiful language is considered to be a painting of the heart and its spiritual significance cannot be ignored. With brush and ink, the calligrapher is able to use a rich variety of form and design to evoke different emotions. As an abstract art, it is akin to music in its harmonious rhythm and movement. In ancient China, writing was reserved for the priestly classes only. Over time, these practitioners evolved into the revered philosophers still studied today, who sought a means of spiritual elevation.

Using calligraphy as a means to enlightenment, the brushwork attempted to capture the essence of the universe and embody the philosophies of all life. If the universe was created from chaos in one stroke, so the universe could be revealed in one stroke of the brush. The concept of oneness became a pivotal idea in Chinese thought. Tao is the belief that everything is linked to one origin, one internal law. Literally meaning 'the Way', Taoist philosophy holds that only humans have the means to stray from oneness. By letting the spirit flow freely through the art of calligraphy, harmony can be achieved. By achieving harmony, our true nature is revealed and the four virtues of benevolence, righteousness, propriety and wisdom will influence our environment.

Kanji characters express their meaning through analogy with nature, at times using several different images to make up one word. For example, the kanji for gentleness combines the symbols for leaf and stream. An image of a small leaf carried effortlessly on the current of quiet stream captures the Tao spirit of gentleness. Love, considered a highly spiritual emotion, is a combination of three symbols that represent the heart surrounded by beauty and graceful movement. The essence of enlightenment expressed by the calligrapher was also present in many other arts and disciplines of ancient China.

Feng Shui – the Art of Harmony and Placement

Feng shui is another art that has been practised in China for thousands of years. This aesthetic of harmony and placement is based on the Taoist belief that all things in the universe contain an ever-present, life-giving force. This omnipresent energy called ch'i must flow freely through the environment in order for all things to benefit from its power. Feng shui acknowledges the

forces of the natural world and provides its practitioners with the means to coexist in tune with the world around them, bringing health, prosperity and happiness into their lives. The cosmic life force of ch'i is a harmonious blend of two energies – yin and yang. Yin is a feminine energy and represents matter. It is shadow, earth and sensitivity. Yang signifies the spirit and masculine energy. It is light, heaven and creativity. These two dynamics do not oppose each other; rather they are complementary forces always balancing each other.

Interpreted in calligraphy, the yin became a broken line and the yang became a solid line. These lines were drawn in different combinations of three called trigrams. The bottom line signified the earth,

The chrysanthemum is one of the four noble plants of China, its layers of golden petals symbolizing the enlightened spirit of hope and the rewards of noble pursuits

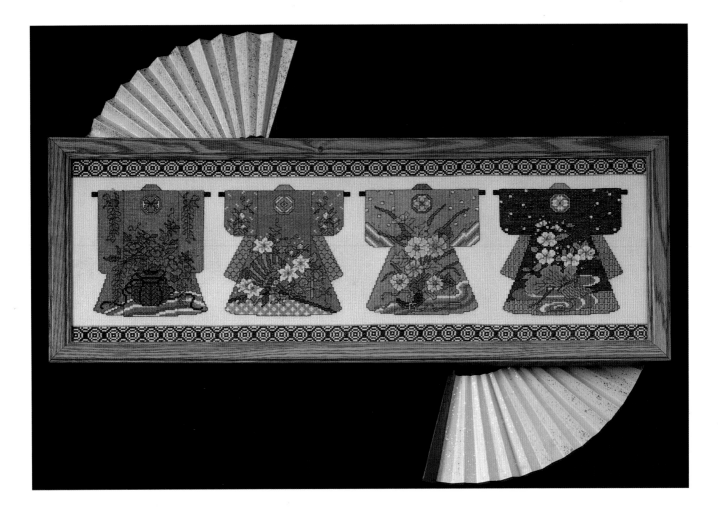

The kimono became a blank canvas on which artists could vividly interpret their love of nature and portray the changing seasons

the top line heaven and the middle line people. Eight trigrams were developed and positioned on a compass called the pa tzu. Feng shui uses this compass to determine the positive or negative ch'i in a designated place. Through understanding the ebb and flow of life, one can use the compass as a guide to alter the space that surrounds them and create a more auspicious environment. The black and white yin yang symbol we are all familiar with, called the t'ai ch'i, expresses the concept of balance perfectly. The black comma shape embraces the white comma shape and vice versa. A small spot of white within the

black yin and a small spot of black within the white yang represent the seed of each side existing in the other. This simple image encompasses the spirit of continuous harmony, the flow of the seasons, and the cycle of human life itself.

Literally meaning wind and water, feng shui is a discipline that moves ch'i by dispersing it in the same way the wind moves falling leaves; and by retaining it the way a river guides the fallen leaves along its course. Taoist belief in the forces of nature includes the importance of the five elements of wood, fire, earth, metal and water. Each element is associated with a direction, colour and quality. The colour green and the east represent Wood. It is expansive and purposeful. Fire is the colour red and its direction is south. It is intuitive and compassionate. Earth is harmonious and loyal. Its direction is the centre and yellow is its colour. Metal is the west. This element is organized, precise and linked to the colour white. Water is the north, imaginative and innovative. Its colour is black. All of us can be identified with one of these elements according to our birth year. Making guided choices in our surroundings in terms of position, colour and materials can create a positive flow of ch'i, thus enhancing the possibilities for a more balanced life.

This short introduction is but a brief taste of the richness of Chinese and Japanese art and culture. It is an endless source of inspiration and I have taken but a small part of that treasure and presented it here. I hope that by creating the designs for this book, I can share with you the mystery and beauty I have discovered in studying the arts of these exotic lands. When you sit down with the projects, close your eyes for a moment and let your senses take you to a place filled with rich symbolism, sumptuous colour, and opulent textures. Let the grace of these enduring cultures run through you and bring a sense of harmony and tranquillity to your own life.

Multiple layers of colour and pattern were carefully chosen when dressing. In this 1859 print by Kunisada, the standing woman is tying a silk obi decorated with stylized floral roundels. (From Matching Pictures with the Chushingura – Act X)

HOW TO USE THIS BOOK

This book is set out in a straightforward way and is easy to use. The projects begin on page 14 and all have a list of materials, stepped instructions and the colour chart needed to complete the embroidery. The charts can be enlarged on a colour photocopier if you like. Zweigart Aida fabrics have mostly been used, with code numbers where relevant. DMC stranded cottons (floss) have been used and those needed for each project are listed in the chart key and assume one skein per colour unless otherwise stated. The stitch counts and design sizes for each design allow for the design *only*, so *do* remember to allow sufficient extra fabric (at least 5cm/2in) around all edges for making up.

At the back of the book, beginning on page 102, is general information on the materials and equipment needed for cross stitch, the preparation and stitching techniques that will help you produce perfect work, and the different ways that the projects have been made up. Metric and imperial measurements are given throughout but are not exactly interchangeable so use either one or the other. Inches has been abbreviated to 'in' throughout.

Oriental Lady Beauty

Inspired by the art of the Japanese print and the exquisite embroidered silks of the Japanese kimono, this design brings together symbolism and colour to capture a spirit of quiet splendour. Delicate blossoms of wisteria hang gracefully, their grape-like scent so powerfully seductive it has been said that sailors far at sea could drink in their sweet aroma long before reaching the shore. Waiting beneath this fragrant shelter is a single figure, the essence of Beauty.

In Edo Japan, a woman's clothing was her principal form of property. Kimono collections became heirlooms, with each generation carefully preserving the precious treasures.

The silky layers of her billowing kimono are dyed in rich violets and mauves, representing strength of beauty, self-knowledge and undying love. Roundels of flowering plum blossoms, the flower of change and renewal, adorn the outer robe. Smaller blossoms scatter across the deep purple obi revealing the ever-present beauty of nature. Kneeling by the edge of the sea, a hint of a smile is revealed from behind the painted fan that Beauty carries. An iridescent dragonfly steals a peak at her loveliness while the sea gently touches her hem in a gesture of life and good fortune. Encircling the figure, a rich gold band encompasses the circle of heaven, and beyond the wisteria is the clear blue of the springtime sky.

DESIGN SIZE: 34.25 x 42cm (13½ x 16½in)
STITCH COUNT: 192w x 231h

MATERIALS
- 46 x 56cm (18 x 22in) Rustico (#54) 14-count Aida
- DMC stranded cotton (floss) as listed in the chart key
- Tapestry needle No.24

1 Begin by referring to Techniques page 103 if necessary. Find and mark the centre of the Aida fabric and then circle the centre of the chart with a pen. Mount your fabric in an embroidery frame if you wish.

2 Begin stitching from the centre of your fabric and work outwards, following the colour changes on the chart. Note: some colours use more than one skein. Work all the cross stitches using two strands of stranded cotton (floss). Work the French knot on the dragonfly with two strands of gold metallic wound once around the needle. Refer to the chart key for working all the backstitches.

3 Once all the stitching is complete, finish your picture by mounting in a suitable frame (see page 106 for advice).

TOP LEFT

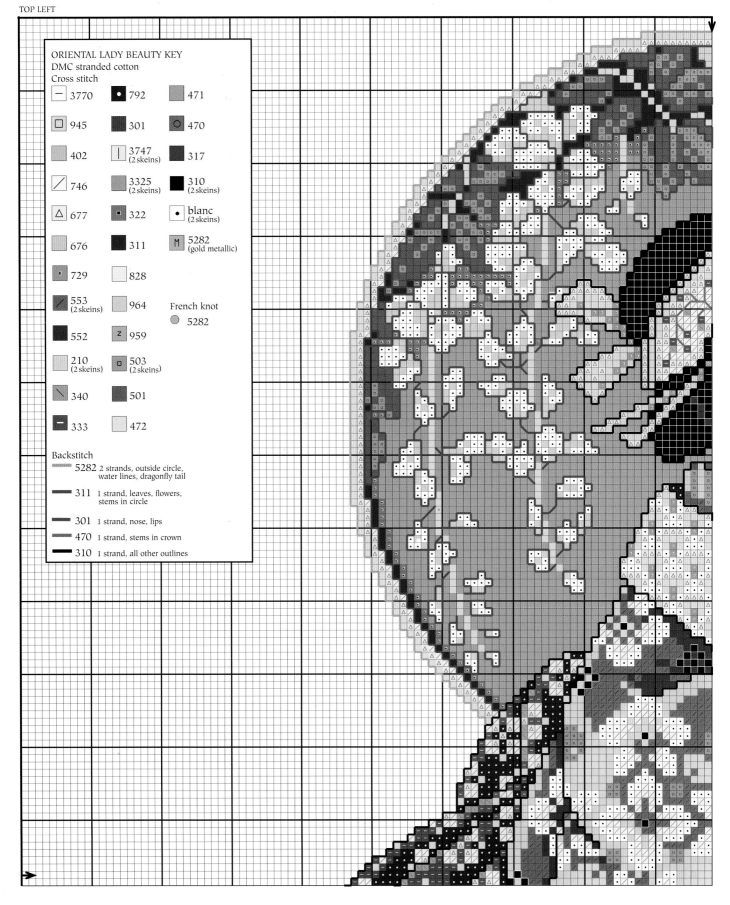

ORIENTAL LADY BEAUTY KEY
DMC stranded cotton
Cross stitch

— 3770	● 792	471
□ 945	301	⊚ 470
402		3747 (2 skeins)	317
╱ 746	3325 (2 skeins)	310 (2 skeins)
△ 677	▣ 322	• blanc (2 skeins)
676	311	M 5282 (gold metallic)
ı 729	828	
╱ 553 (2 skeins)	964	**French knot**
552	z 959	◯ 5282
210 (2 skeins)	▢ 503 (2 skeins)	
╲ 340	501	
▬ 333	472	

Backstitch

▬▬▬ 5282 2 strands, outside circle, water lines, dragonfly tail

▬▬▬ 311 1 strand, leaves, flowers, stems in circle

▬▬▬ 301 1 strand, nose, lips

▬▬▬ 470 1 strand, stems in crown

▬▬▬ 310 1 strand, all other outlines

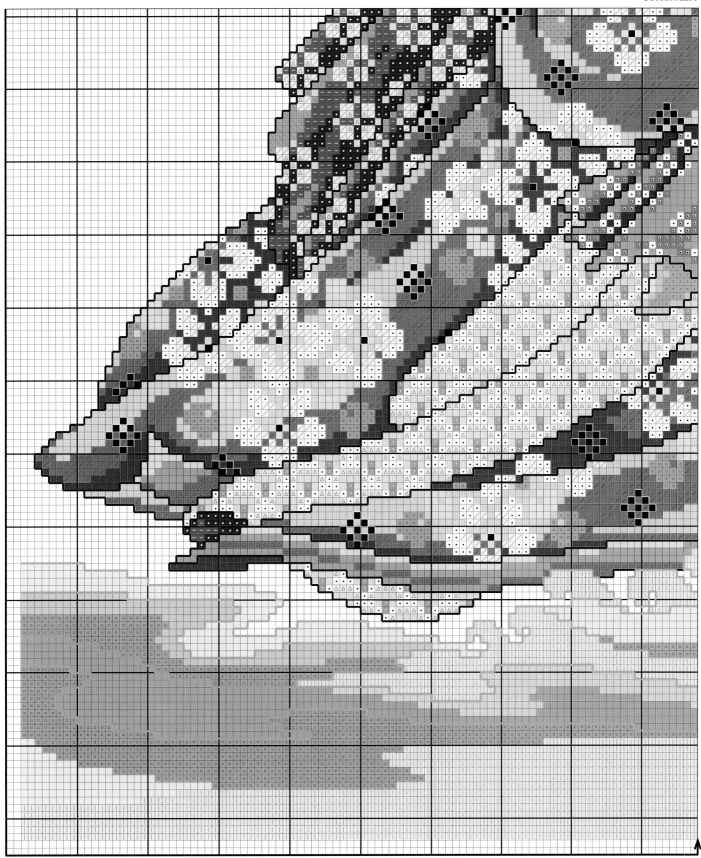

ORIENTAL LADY BEAUTY

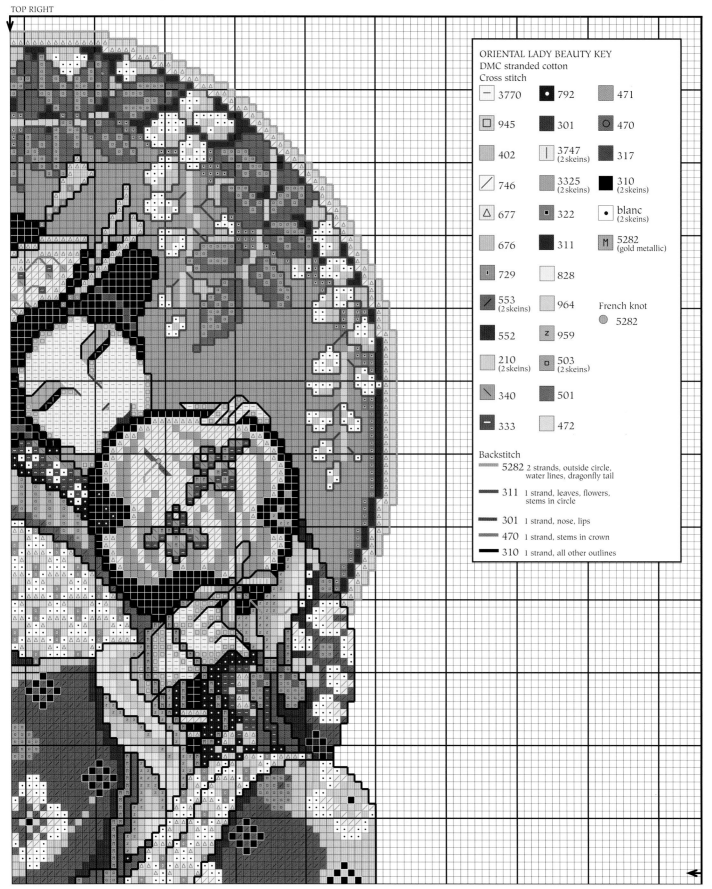

ORIENTAL LADY BEAUTY KEY
DMC stranded cotton
Cross stitch

− 3770	• 792	471
945	301	470
402	3747 (2 skeins)	317
╱ 746	3325 (2 skeins)	310 (2 skeins)
△ 677	322	• blanc (2 skeins)
676	311	M 5282 (gold metallic)
729	828	
553 (2 skeins)	964	French knot
552	z 959	5282
210 (2 skeins)	503 (2 skeins)	
340	501	
− 333	472	

Backstitch

5282 2 strands, outside circle, water lines, dragonfly tail

311 1 strand, leaves, flowers, stems in circle

301 1 strand, nose, lips

470 1 strand, stems in crown

310 1 strand, all other outlines

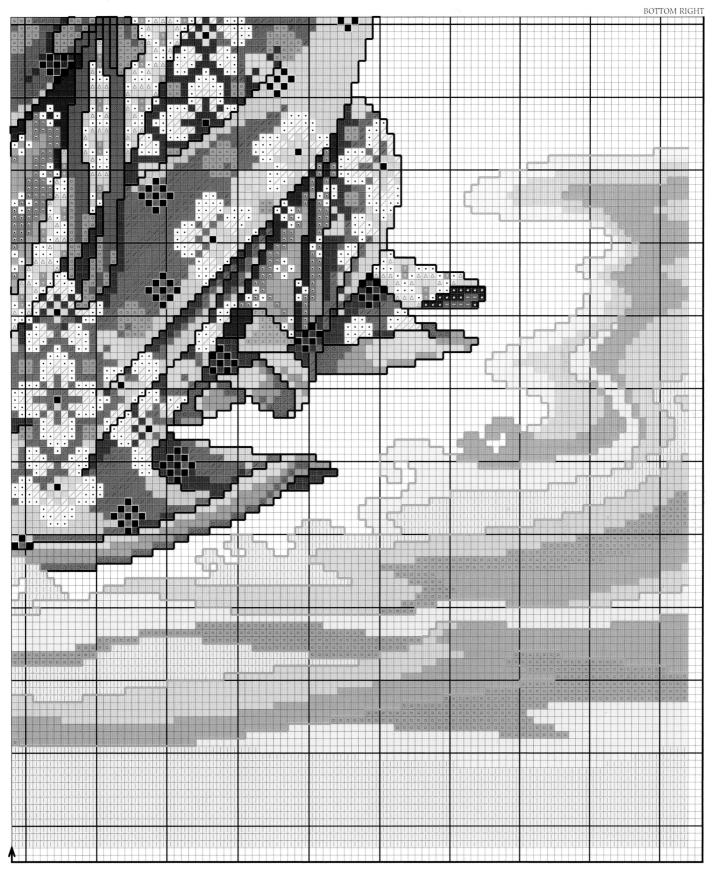

Gifts of the Orient

Feng shui, the ancient Chinese art of harmonious placement, teaches us that all things have a balance. The yin is the receptive, feminine side, and the yang is the active, masculine side. These two designs, featuring the poppy and panda, are rich in feng shui symbolism.

Feng shui has been practised in china for thousands of years. This aesthetic of harmony and placement is based on the Taoist belief that all things in the universe contain an ever-present, life-giving force. This omnipresent energy, called ch'i, must flow freely through the environment in order for all things to benefit from its power.

Oriental poppies are flowers that instantly bring us to an exotic world, with their shimmering, ruffled petals drenched with colour. The Chinese character for tranquillity is placed in the lower left-hand corner, representing harmonious relationships and peace in the heart. The broad, silky flowers of the poppy are the forceful, creative energy of the spirit. The soft blue-green of the rounded bowl is the gentle, responsive energy of the earth and together they bring a delicate balance to this design.

The panda is a highly treasured animal in China. Ancient emperors kept giant pandas in captivity, where it was believed they were capable of warding off disaster and evil spirits. In a shady bamboo grove the panda feasts happily on his favourite dish. The motion and music of the swaying canes, a symbol of longevity and courage, surround him as the life force of ch'i flows freely in the breeze. The panda's black and white coat brings to mind the complementary forces of yin and yang and the harmony they create together.

The panda design has been made up into a sachet to hold pot-pourri but would also make a lovely card. Simply stitch the design and mount it into a ready-made card with a minimum aperture of 6.5 x 9cm (2¹/₂ x 3¹/₂in)

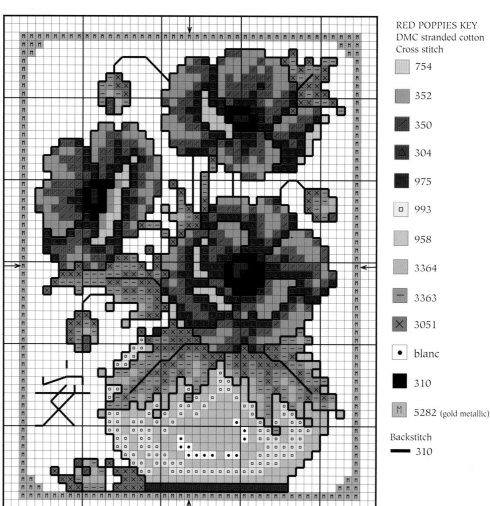

RED POPPIES KEY
DMC stranded cotton
Cross stitch

754
352
350
304
975
993
958
3364
3363
3051
blanc
310
M	5282 (gold metallic)

Backstitch
— 310

RED POPPIES BAG

In this design, the traditional scarlet poppy puts on a gorgeous show, while a simple celadon bowl complements the arrangement. The design is used to create a delicate drawstring jewellery bag. Finished in red silk, it's perfect for trinkets or to give as a gift.

DESIGN SIZE: 6 x 8cm (2⅜ x 3in)
STITCH COUNT: 43w x 57h

MATERIALS
• 13 x 18cm (5 x 7in) Rustico (#54) 18-count Aida
• DMC stranded cotton (floss) as in chart key
• Tapestry needle No.24

1 Begin by referring to Techniques, page 103 if necessary. Find and mark the centre of the Aida fabric and circle the centre of the chart with a pen. Mount your fabric in an embroidery frame if you wish.

2 Begin stitching from the centre of your fabric and work outwards, following the colour changes on the chart. Work all the cross stitches using two strands of stranded cotton (floss). Work the backstitch outlining using one strand of black and the Chinese symbol using two strands.

3 When all the embroidery is completed, the work can be made up into a drawstring bag (see page 105).

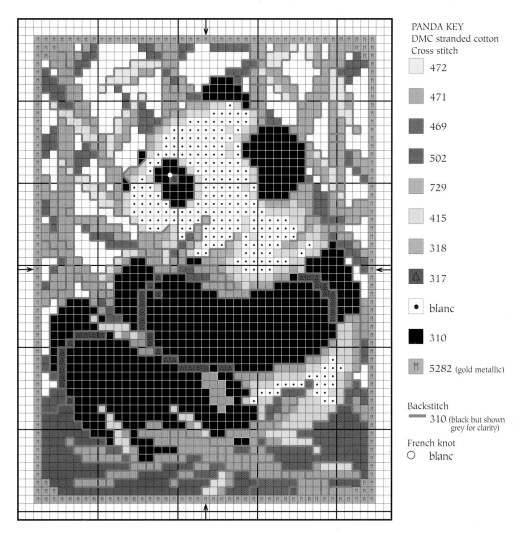

PANDA KEY
DMC stranded cotton
Cross stitch

	472
	471
	469
	502
	729
	415
	318
△	317
•	blanc
■	310
M	5282 (gold metallic)

Backstitch
—— 310 (black but shown grey for clarity)

French knot
○ blanc

PANDA SACHET

This endearing panda design is used to create a small sachet filled with your favourite pot-pourri.

Hung from a drawer pull or a bedpost, this little treasure will bring a smile to your heart each time you see it.

Mounted on rich brocade and trimmed with golden cord and a tassel, it also makes a lovely hostess gift.

DESIGN SIZE: 6 x 8cm (2⅜ x 3in)
STITCH COUNT: 43w x 57h

MATERIALS
• 13 x 18cm (5 x 7in) Rustico (#54) 18-count Aida
• DMC stranded cotton (floss) as in chart key
• Tapestry needle No.24

1 Begin by referring to Techniques, page 103 if necessary. Find and mark the centre of the Aida fabric and circle the centre of the chart with a pen. Mount your fabric in an embroidery frame if you wish.

2 Begin stitching from the centre of your fabric and work outwards, following the colour changes on the chart. Work all the cross stitches using two strands of stranded cotton (floss). Work the French knot in the eye with two strands of white, wound twice around the needle. Work the black backstitch outlines using one strand (shown in grey on the chart for clarity).

3 When all the embroidery is completed, the work can be made up into a scented sachet (see page 108).

Four Elements

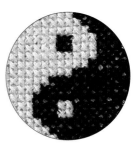

Water, Fire, Earth and Wood are the four elements that provide the inspiration for these elegant embroideries.

The characteristic strength of Wood is seen in the tall, slender stalks of bamboo with their dancing green leaves. The kanji symbol for wisdom reflects the philosophies of the East, belief in knowledge and the power of enlightenment.

The deep reds of ripening berries and plums hold the nature of Fire. The symbol for prosperity gathers the energy of the element, just as the southern sun fills the day with a bounty of warmth and radiant light.

The Chinese symbol for balance captures the essence of Earth. Tao theory says that earth's direction is centre, signifying balance and symmetry. Golden yellow chrysanthemums glow in hope and open movement, bringing a flow of positive ch'i to our lives.

The ancient art of feng shui maintains that there is a universal life force that flows through all things. The embracing commas of the t'ai ch'i circle symbolize the complementary forces of nature in eternal harmony, each side giving life to the other. The black yin, the spirit of the feminine, is earth and shadow. The white yang is the masculine essence, representing heaven and light. The trigram at the top of each design represents the spirit of different elements of nature.

The character for longevity contains the spirit of Water. The constant life force of ch'i is directed by the water's eternal flow. The blue-violets and greens of the night-blooming water lily signify the cool colour palette of the north and hold the promise of long, harmonious relationships.

Trigrams are figures consisting of three lines developed from Chinese script for the complementary energies of yin and yang.

A broken line represents yin and a solid line is yang. These are combined to form three-line symbols or trigrams, as shown:

chen	Li	K'un	K'an
green	red	yellow	blue
wood	fire	earth	water
east	south	centre	north
spring	summer	autumn	winter

24

BAMBOO 'WISDOM'

Chen is the trigram for Wood. Its two broken lines above a lower solid line represent feminine energy and its underlying masculine qualities. It is a combination of earthly endeavours and spiritual enlightenment that brings us wisdom. The long, earth-bound stems of the bamboo securely hold leaves the green colour of new life.

DESIGN SIZE: 15.25 x 20.3cm (6 x 8in)
STITCH COUNT: 84w x 112h

MATERIALS
• 28 x 33cm (11 x 13in) Rustico (#54) 14-count Aida
• DMC stranded cotton (floss) as listed in the chart key
• Tapestry needle No.24

1 Begin by referring to Techniques, page 103 if necessary. Find and mark the centre of the fabric and then circle the centre of the chart with a pen. Mount your fabric in an embroidery frame if you wish.

2 Begin stitching from the centre of your fabric and work outwards, following the colour changes on the chart. Work all the cross stitches using two strands of stranded cotton (floss). Refer to the chart key for working all the backstitches.

3 Once all the stitching is complete, finish your picture by mounting in a suitable frame.

BAMBOO 'WISDOM' KEY
DMC stranded cotton
Cross stitch

z	677		869		470	•	blanc
□	676		472		3814	M	5282 (gold metallic)
	729	/	471		310		

Backstitch
5282 2 strands, wisdom symbol outline & both sides of black border
3814 1 strand, leaves and bamboo outlines
310 1 strand, trigram outline, around yin yang symbol & outside green border
470 1 strand, pattern below trigram & above yin yang symbol

Plum 'Prosperity'

Li, the trigram for Fire, is composed of one broken line between two solid lines, showing the feminine component inside the element's masculine energy. The seeds of the abundant red berries and ripening plums continue the cycle of life, just as the yang contains the seed of the yin, creating a harmonious flow of energy and opening the door to prosperity.

Design Size: 15.25 x 20.3cm (6 x 8in)
Stitch Count: 84w x 112h

MATERIALS

- 28 x 33cm (11 x 13in) Rustico (#54) 14-count Aida
- DMC stranded cotton (floss) as listed in the chart key
- Tapestry needle No.24

1 Begin by referring to Techniques, page 103 if necessary. Find and mark the centre of the fabric and then circle the centre of the chart with a pen. Mount your fabric in an embroidery frame if you wish.

2 Begin stitching from the centre of your fabric and work outwards, following the colour changes on the chart. Work all the cross stitches using two strands of stranded cotton (floss). Refer to the chart key for working all the backstitches.

3 Once all the stitching is complete, finish your picture by mounting in a suitable frame.

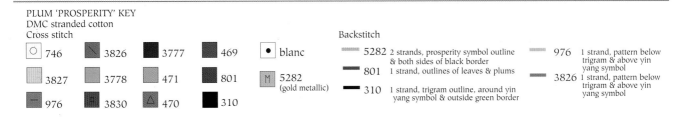

PLUM 'PROSPERITY' KEY
DMC stranded cotton
Cross stitch

○ 746	3826	3777	469
3827	3778	471	801
976	3830	470	310

• blanc

M 5282 (gold metallic)

Backstitch

5282 2 strands, prosperity symbol outline & both sides of black border
801 1 strand, outlines of leaves & plums
310 1 strand, trigram outline, around yin yang symbol & outside green border
976 1 strand, pattern below trigram & above yin yang symbol
3826 1 strand, pattern below trigram & above yin yang symbol

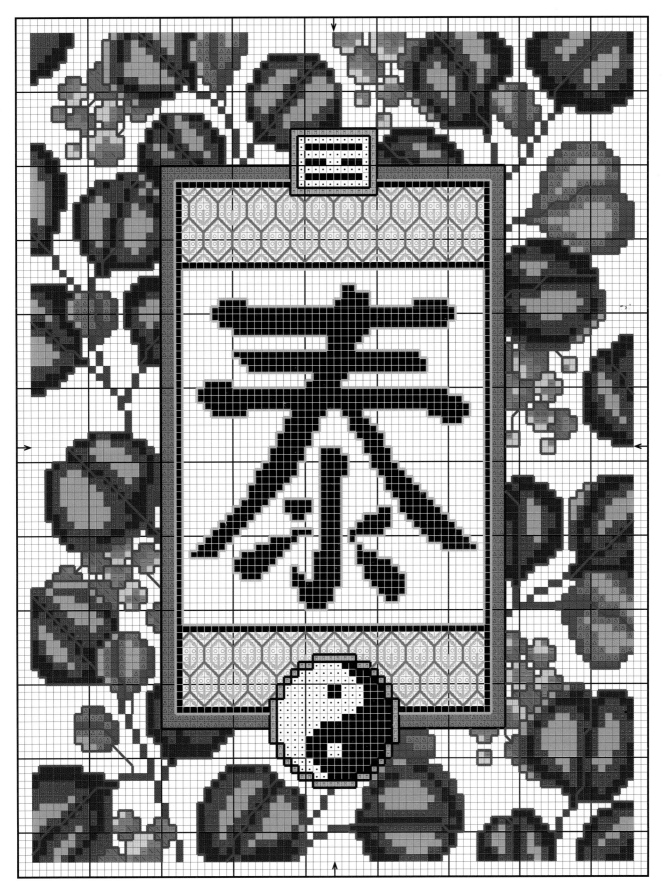

CHRYSANTHEMUM 'BALANCE'

K'un, the trigram for Earth, consists of three broken lines, making it a decidedly feminine element. The yellow chrysanthemum provides the spirit of higher wisdom creating the ideal balance. These flowers are some of the latest to bloom in the garden, often seen peeking through a dusting of early winter snow.

DESIGN SIZE: 15.25 x 20.3cm (6 x 8in)
STITCH COUNT: 84w x 112h

MATERIALS

- 28 x 33cm (11 x 13in) Rustico (#54) 14-count Aida
- DMC stranded cotton (floss) as listed in the chart key
- Tapestry needle No.24

1 Begin by referring to Techniques, page 103 if necessary. Find and mark the centre of the fabric and then circle the centre of the chart with a pen. Mount your fabric in an embroidery frame if you wish.

2 Begin stitching from the centre of your fabric and work outwards, following the colour changes on the chart. Work all the cross stitches using two strands of stranded cotton (floss). Refer to the chart key for working all the backstitches.

3 Once all the stitching is complete, finish your picture by mounting in a suitable frame.

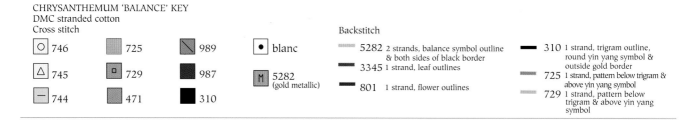

CHRYSANTHEMUM 'BALANCE' KEY
DMC stranded cotton
Cross stitch

⊙ 746	725	989
△ 745	▫ 729	987
− 744	471	310
• blanc		
M 5282 (gold metallic)		

Backstitch

5282	2 strands, balance symbol outline & both sides of black border
3345	1 strand, leaf outlines
801	1 strand, flower outlines
310	1 strand, trigram outline, round yin yang symbol & outside gold border
725	1 strand, pattern below trigram & above yin yang symbol
729	1 strand, pattern below trigram & above yin yang symbol

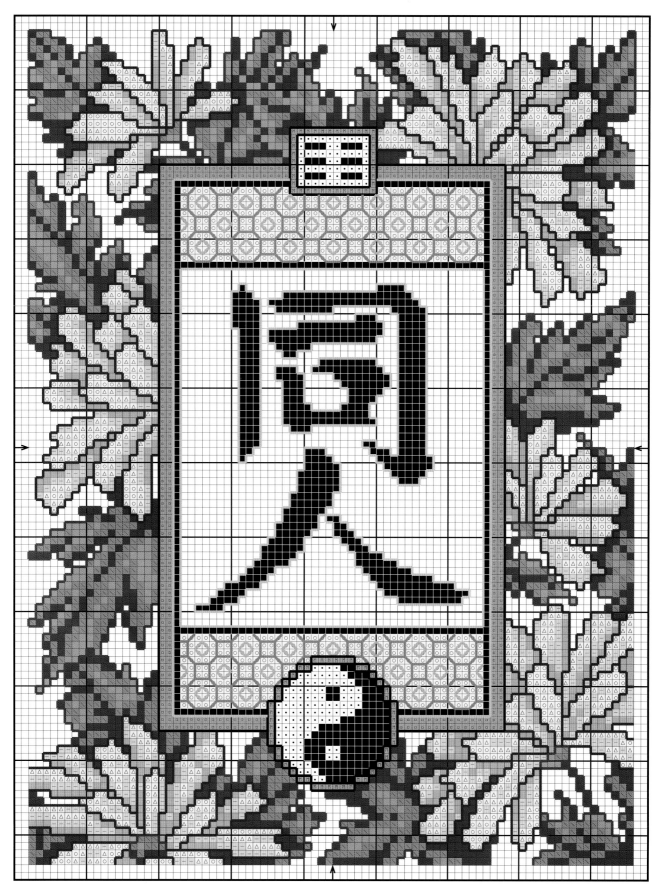

WATER LILY 'LONGEVITY'

K'an, the trigram for Water, consists of a solid centre line with broken lines above and below, indicating the masculine qualities within the feminine spirit. The water lily or lotus is the eternal symbol of perfect beauty and the first flower mentioned in world literature.

DESIGN SIZE: 15.25 x 20.3cm (6 x 8in)
STITCH COUNT: 84w x 112h

MATERIALS

- 28 x 33cm (11 x 13in) Rustico (#54) 14-count Aida
- DMC stranded cotton (floss) as listed in the chart key
- Tapestry needle No.24

1 Begin by referring to Techniques page 103 if necessary. Find and mark the centre of the fabric and then circle the centre of the chart with a pen. Mount your fabric in an embroidery frame if you wish.

2 Begin stitching from the centre of your fabric and work outwards, following the colour changes on the chart. Work all the cross stitches using two strands of stranded cotton (floss). Refer to the chart key for working all the backstitches.

3 Once all the stitching is complete, finish your picture by mounting in a suitable frame.

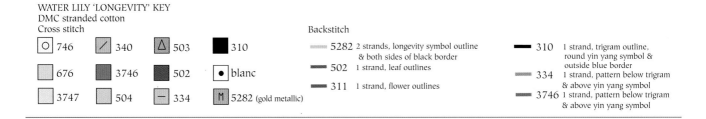

WATER LILY 'LONGEVITY' KEY
DMC stranded cotton

Cross stitch

O 746	/ 340	△ 503	■ 310
676	3746	502	• blanc
3747	504	– 334	M 5282 (gold metallic)

Backstitch

5282 2 strands, longevity symbol outline & both sides of black border
502 1 strand, leaf outlines
311 1 strand, flower outlines

310 1 strand, trigram outline, round yin yang symbol & outside blue border
334 1 strand, pattern below trigram & above yin yang symbol
3746 1 strand, pattern below trigram & above yin yang symbol

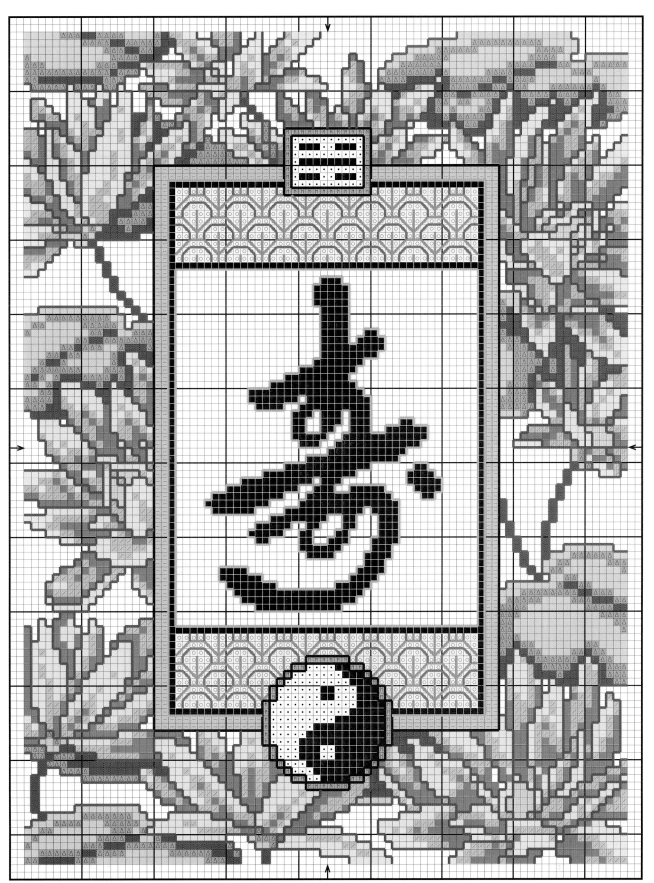

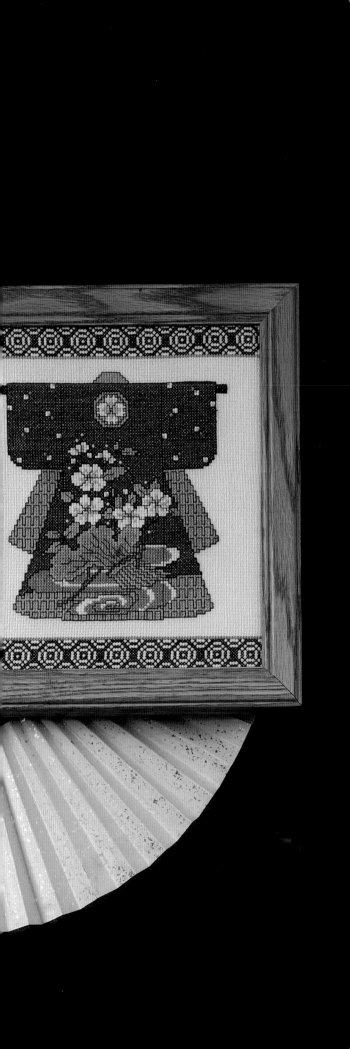

Kimono Row

In this design, a row of kimonos creates an artistic display of the four seasons.

With April snow still on the ground, an intricately woven basket filled with peonies and wisteria heralds spring. The warm peach background surrounds the leaves and tendrils like the promise of a June breeze.

A clear blue summer sky is the backdrop for the next kimono, with pink clematis blooms twining around a bamboo trellis and fan. Traditional geometric patterns the rosy colour of an August sunset complete the design.

Chrysanthemums are noble flowers of the autumn garden. Here, their pink petals and celadon leaves are set against a golden background that holds the last warmth of the passing season, while blue waves hint at approaching winter.

The final kimono has tiny white petals falling like snowflakes against the deep blue of a winter's twilight, while a stream runs beneath the ice. Plum blossoms are the first flowers to open in late winter. Surviving the harshest weather, they hold the spirit of growth and renewal.

程 *The Kimono embodies the spirit of the orient in a beautiful balance of art and design. opulent embroideries, age-old dyeing techniques and delicately rendered painting were all used to embellish these luxurious garments.*

The kimono has endured as a symbol of beauty and grace through centuries of Japanese cultural history. Once an everyday symbol of the owner's wealth and good fortune, in modern times these exquisite garments are more often reserved for special occasions and celebrations. The wedding kimono and the child's kimono, pictured below and on the opposite page, are perfect examples of the wonderful art of the kimono still in evidence today. Each fabric was created for the specific wearer. The symbolism of nature and the celebration of life are artistically incorporated into the garments. Drawing inspiration from these and other kimonos, the Kimono Row embroidery adapts their rich colour and symbolism, to depict the changing seasons and the glory of nature.

The kimono was a blank canvas for artists on which they could express the beauty of the natural world. This traditional silk wedding kimono, called a furisode, is decorated with cranes for longevity, royal carriages for celebration and colourful flowers of every season. The flowing lines of the stream carry the eternal life force and hopes for a life of peace and harmony

DESIGN SIZE: 66 x 23cm (9 x 26in)
STITCH COUNT: 364w x 126h

MATERIALS

- 33 x 76cm (13 x 30in) white 14-count Aida
- DMC stranded cotton (floss) as in chart key
- Tapestry needle No.24

1 Begin by referring to Techniques, page 103 if necessary. Find and mark the centre of the Aida fabric and circle the centre of the chart with a pen. Mount your fabric in an embroidery frame if you wish.

2 Begin stitching from the centre of your fabric and work outwards, following the colour changes on the chart. Note: some colours use more than one skein. Work all the cross stitches using two strands of stranded cotton (floss) and the black backstitch outlining using one strand.

3 Once all the stitching is complete, finish your picture by mounting in a suitable frame (see page 106).

This vintage child's kimono made of brightly coloured silk was probably worn on a festive occasion such as a birthday. The cheerful, tasselled bells are a symbol of celebration, while the double crane pattern wishes the wearer a long life

KIMONO ROW KEY
DMC stranded cotton
Cross stitch

3668
(2 skeins)

961
(2 skeins)

340

333

783
(4 skeins)

976
(2 skeins)

420

838

794

799

796
(2 skeins)

931
(2 skeins)

453

503

732

471

3363

823
(3 skeins)

blanc
(2 skeins)

Backstitch
310

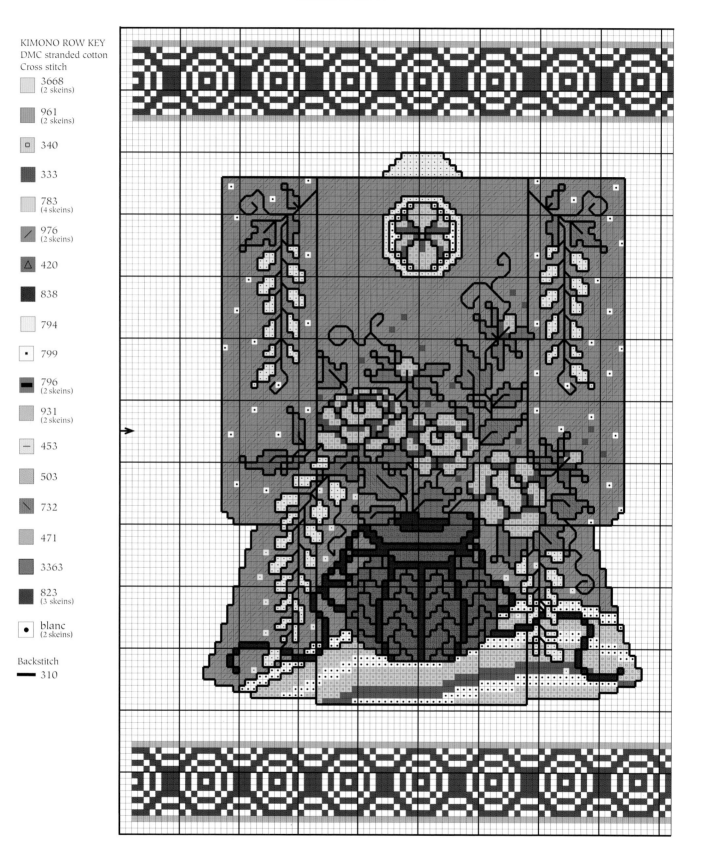

KIMONO ROW KEY
DMC stranded cotton
Cross stitch

3668
(2 skeins)

961
(2 skeins)

340

333

783
(4 skeins)

976
(2 skeins)

420

838

794

799

796
(2 skeins)

931
(2 skeins)

453

503

732

471

3363

823
(3 skeins)

blanc
(2 skeins)

Backstitch

310

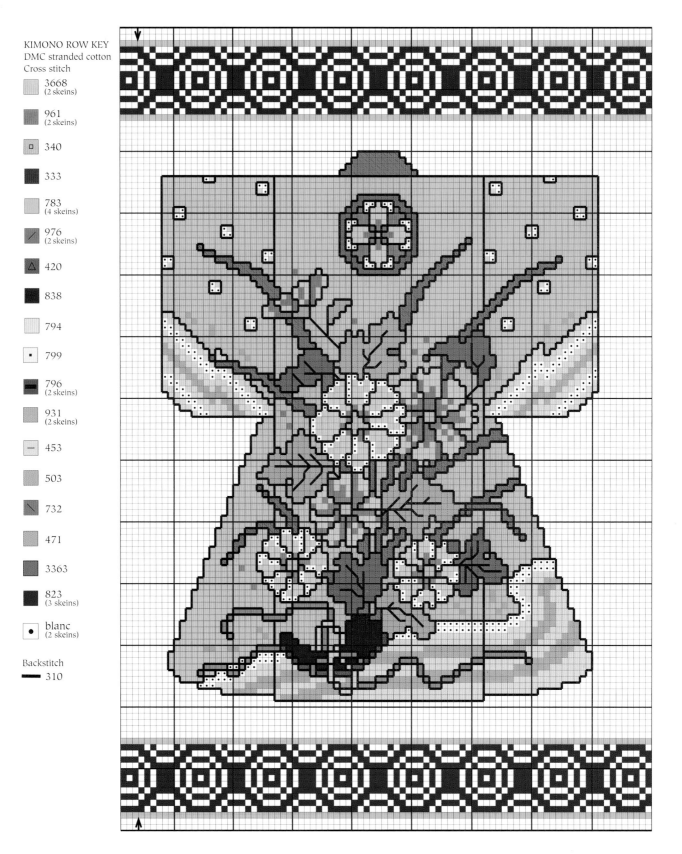

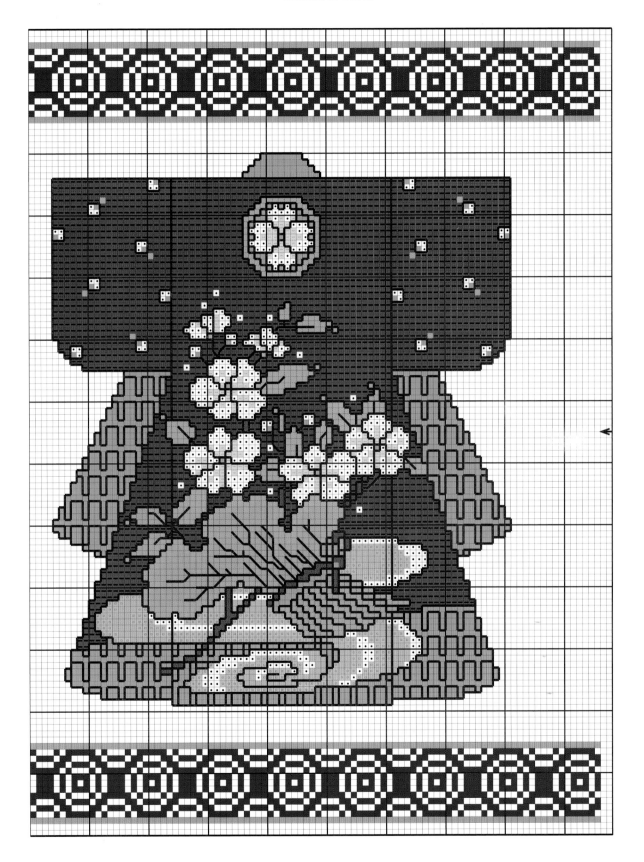

Little Treasures

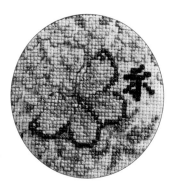

One of the most significant qualities of Chinese and Japanese art is its ability to bring the spirit of nature indoors. The art of pun-sai first appeared in China over a thousand years ago. It was introduced to Japan early in the twelfth century through Zen Buddhist monks and took on the name of bonsai. Bonsai was practised amongst the priestly and ruling classes and quickly became a symbol of prestige and honour. It represents a fusion of meditation and expression, symbolizing the virtues of truth, goodness and beauty.

Calligraphy is a sacred art form in china and it is said that the practice should take place only in moments of calm and tranquillity. This incomparably beautiful language is considered to be a painting of the heart with great spiritual significance. with brush and ink, the calligrapher uses a rich variety of form and design to evoke different emotions.

The largest design in this group of wooden trinket bowls features a classically shaped porcelain planter with a cobalt blue glaze housing a juniper tree, carefully tended for many years. The kanji symbol for eternity echoes nature's ever-present spirit.

The motif for the medium-sized bowl lid captures the moment when a blue copper butterfly alights on the drooping branch of a flowering cherry tree, blossoms showering down in the spring breeze. The Chinese calligraphic character for revelation defines the inspiring scene.

The smallest of the three lids carries its own tiny treasure: a shimmering dragonfly gliding into view. Beside it, the calligraphic symbol for gentleness suggests the good will of a soft summer breeze.

This traditional bonsai design can also be made up into a small, rounded sachet or pincushion edged in gold braid, making a delightful gift for a fellow cross stitcher!

BUTTERFLY 'REVELATION'

The cherry blossom is Japan's most celebrated flower and each year announces the arrival of spring. Most fragrant in the early morning sun, clouds of pink blooms fill the landscape. The character for revelation signifies the beauty revealed from heaven above.

DESIGN SIZE: 7 x 7cm (2¾ x 2¾in)
STITCH COUNT: 50w x 49h

MATERIALS

- 18 x 18cm (7 x 7in) ivory 18-count Aida
- DMC stranded cotton (floss) as listed in the chart key
- Tapestry needle No.24
- Wooden trinket bowl (#W3E from Framecraft, see Suppliers page 111)

DRAGONFLY 'GENTLENESS'

In the practice of feng shui, the idea of ease and gentleness refers to the smooth flow of energy through our environment, much the way a running stream influences the destiny of the fallen leaf, or a dragonfly drifts on the summer wind.

DESIGN SIZE: 3.5 x 3.5cm (1³⁄₁₆ x 1³⁄₁₆in)
STITCH COUNT: 25w x 25h

MATERIALS

- 13 x 13cm (5 x 5in) ivory 18-count Aida
- DMC stranded cotton (floss) as listed in the chart key
- Tapestry needle No.24
- Wooden trinket bowl (#W1E from Framecraft, see Suppliers page 111)

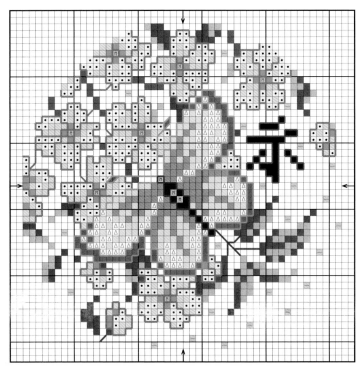

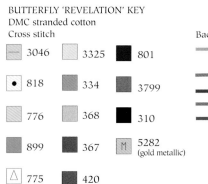

BUTTERFLY 'REVELATION' KEY
DMC stranded cotton
Cross stitch

─ 3046	3325	■ 801
• 818	334	3799
776	368	■ 310
899	367	M 5282 (gold metallic)
△ 775	420	

Backstitch
- ── 3799 1 strand, butterfly wings & antennae
- ── 3722 1 strand, around flowers
- ── 367 1 strand, leaf stems
- ── 420 1 strand, stems
- ── 310 1 strand of black, parts of butterfly body & around symbol

DRAGONFLY 'GENTLENESS' KEY
DMC stranded cotton
Cross stitch

+ 3046	311
964	M 5282 (gold metallic)
959	
958	
519	
518	

Backstitch
- ── 310
- ── 311

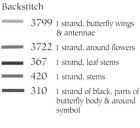

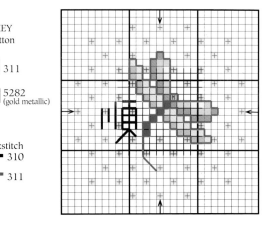

BONSAI 'ETERNITY'

A carefully tended bonsai tree can live for hundreds of years, becoming a family treasure handed down from generation to generation. The annual rings of the tree reflect the time devoted to its care, the task a pleasure and source of inner peace.

DESIGN SIZE: 7.6 x 7.6cm (3 x 3in)
STITCH COUNT: 55w x 55h

MATERIALS

- 18 x 18cm (7 x 7in) ivory 18-count Aida
- DMC stranded cotton (floss) as listed in the chart key
- Tapestry needle No.24
- Wooden trinket bowl (#W4E from Framecraft, see Suppliers page 111)

1 Begin by referring to Techniques page 103 if necessary. Find and mark the centre of the fabric and circle the centre of the chart with a pen.

2 Begin stitching from the centre of your fabric and work outwards, following the colour changes on the chart.

For Butterfly 'Revelation': Work the cross stitches using two strands of stranded cotton (floss). Refer to the chart key to work the backstitches and outlines.

For Dragonfly 'Gentleness': Work the cross stitches using two strands of stranded cotton (floss). Use one strand to work the backstitches and outlines in black and blue as shown, and use two strands to backstitch the symbol.

For Bonsai 'Eternity': Work all cross stitches and blue French knot on the dragonfly using two strands of stranded cotton (floss). Using one strand, work the blue and black backstitch outlines (the black is shown as a dark grey on the chart for clarity).

3 Once complete, mount the embroidery in a trinket bowl lid following the manufacturer's instructions.

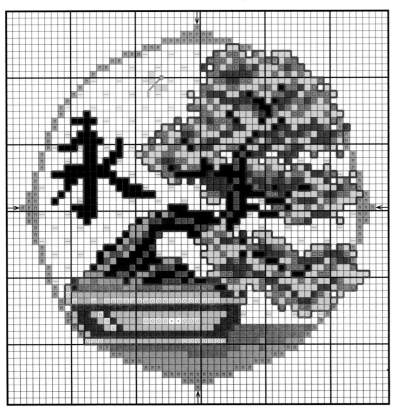

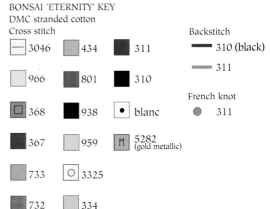

BONSAI 'ETERNITY' KEY
DMC stranded cotton

Cross stitch

		Backstitch
3046	434	311	— 310 (black)
966	801	310	— 311
368	938	• blanc	French knot
367	959	M 5282 (gold metallic)	● 311
733	O 3325		
732	334		

Oriental Lady Grace

The delicate green leaves of a willow gently blowing in the warmth of an early summer breeze; a small bird perching on the finger of a woman dressed in a sumptuous silk kimono embroidered with glorious peonies – all these things combine to make a sublime picture of Grace.

The obi, a sash worn around the waist, developed into an elaborate accessory to the kimono. Intricate pattern and decoration adorned the obi and complex methods of tying them were fashioned to show them off to best advantage.

The Japanese wood block prints from the late eighteenth and early nineteenth century and the design sense of the Art Nouveau period are strong influences on the simple composition and flowing lines in this design. The circle, representing the spirit of heaven, frames the figure with boughs of green willow, showing graceful movement against a soft blue sky. Flowers can evoke symbolic meanings, the changing seasons, or simply the beauty of nature. The elegant blooms of tree peonies can fill an early summer garden with a spectacular display, with as many as fifty flowers carried on a mature plant. Here, the kimono is brimming with pink buds and blossoms set on a golden background to bring a warmth and richness to the design. In kimono fashion, the obi and inner layers of the kimono were often made in small geometric and striped patterns dyed in colours to complement the outer robe. A soft aqua with traditional patterns is used in these areas. The overall mood of this picture is meant to bring a feeling of ease and contentment.

DESIGN SIZE: 33 x 42cm (13 x 16½in)
STITCH COUNT: 182w x 232h

MATERIALS
- 46 x 56cm (18 x 22in) Rustico (#54) 14-count Aida
- DMC stranded cotton (floss) as listed in the chart key
- Tapestry needle No.24

1 Begin by referring to Techniques, page 103, if necessary. Find and mark the centre of the Aida fabric and then circle the centre of the chart with a pen. Mount your fabric in an embroidery frame if you wish.

2 Start stitching from the fabric centre and work outwards, following the colour changes on the chart. (Some colours use more than one skein.) Work all the cross stitches and black French knots using two strands of stranded cotton (floss). Refer to the chart key for working all the backstitches.

3 Once all the stitching is complete, finish your picture by mounting in a suitable frame (see page 106 for advice).

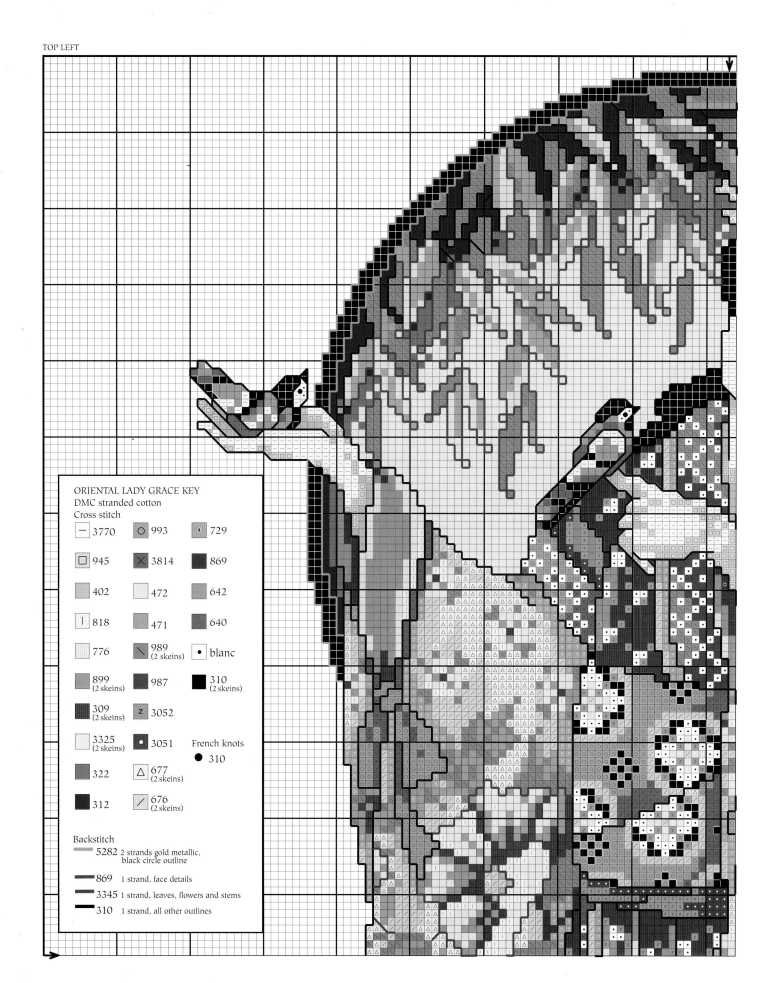

ORIENTAL LADY GRACE KEY
DMC stranded cotton
Cross stitch

— 3770	⊙ 993	729
▣ 945	✕ 3814	869
402	472	642
I 818	471	640
776	＼ 989 (2 skeins)	• blanc
899 (2 skeins)	987	310 (2 skeins)
309 (2 skeins)	z 3052	
3325 (2 skeins)	3051	French knots • 310
322	△ 677 (2 skeins)	
312	／ 676 (2 skeins)	

Backstitch
5282 2 strands gold metallic, black circle outline
869 1 strand, face details
3345 1 strand, leaves, flowers and stems
310 1 strand, all other outlines

49

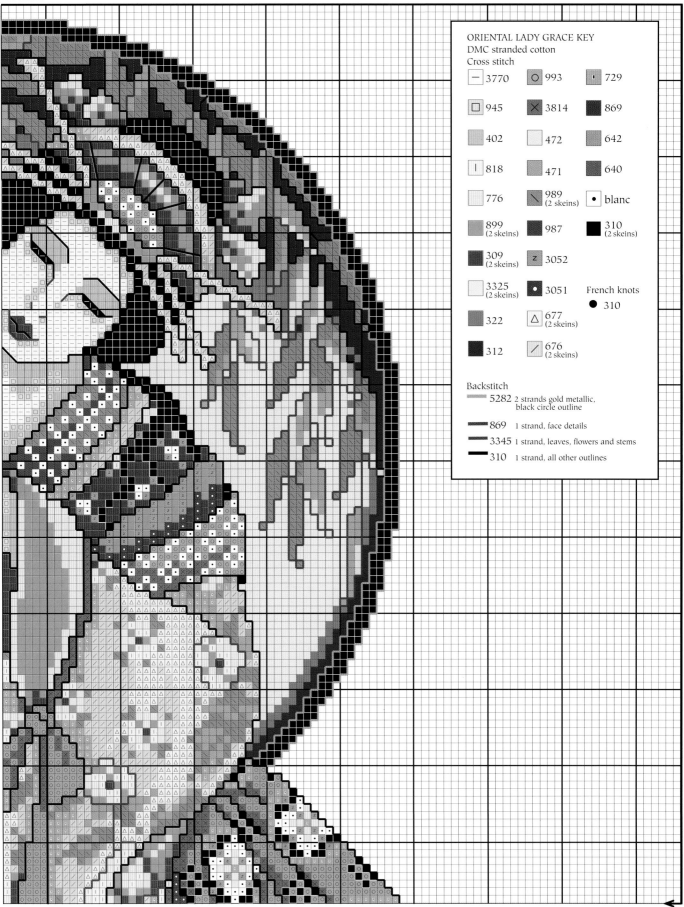

ORIENTAL LADY GRACE KEY
DMC stranded cotton
Cross stitch

− 3770	◎ 993	∙ 729
☐ 945	✕ 3814	869
402	472	642
ǀ 818	471	640
776	╲ 989 (2 skeins)	• blanc
899 (2 skeins)	987	310 (2 skeins)
309 (2 skeins)	z 3052	
3325 (2 skeins)	⊡ 3051	French knots
322	△ 677 (2 skeins)	● 310
312	╱ 676 (2 skeins)	

Backstitch

5282 2 strands gold metallic, black circle outline

869 1 strand, face details

3345 1 strand, leaves, flowers and stems

310 1 strand, all other outlines

Floral Wall Hanging

程 *Chinese and Japanese hanging scrolls, painted on continuous lengths of paper or silk, often depicted sweeping landscapes, scenes from nature or vivid renderings of birds and flowers. Gilded backgrounds added to the beauty of the finished piece. The completed scrolls were mounted and bordered with richly embroidered or block-printed silks of subtle pattern and colour.*

Flowers hold special significance in cultures throughout the world. Their delicate petals carry our messages of love, joy, caring and comfort to those that receive them. In endless variation, the miracle of life is seen from the first planting of the seed in the spring, to the opening of the blossoms, and finally the return to seed again.

Three delightful floral designs grace this sumptuous wall hanging. Morning glories, orchids and irises, each with their own symbolic significance, have captured the imagination of artists for centuries. Traditionally, the Chinese use flowers to evoke feelings of goodness and well-being. Mounted on a rich blue brocade of plum blossoms and bamboo, these flowers bring the joyful spirit of the garden indoors.

The sky-blue morning glories with their heart-shaped leaves greet the day with a sweet kiss of affection, their tendrils climbing towards the heavens.

The exotic orchid is one of the four noble plants of China. Its alluring petals symbolize friendship and sincerity while the heady scent carries the promise of beauty and love.

When the last chill of winter past gives way to the rebirth of spring, the Siberian iris unfolds its velvet flowers to the sun in a gesture of hope and faith.

The delicate flowers of the morning glory have earned them the name of 'Heavenly Blue'. They carry a message of hope and possibility. Express these heartfelt sentiments to someone by placing this design into a ready-made card

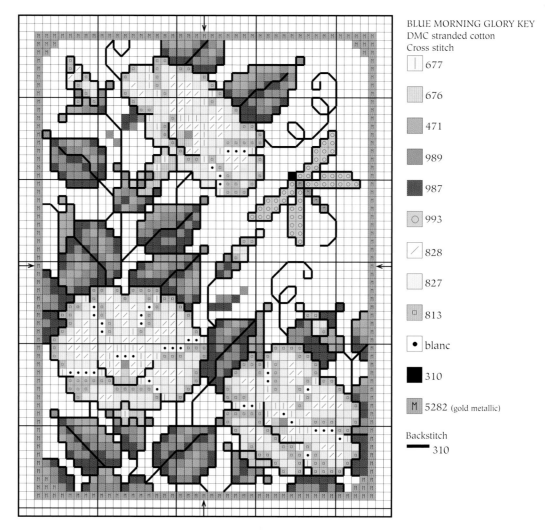

BLUE MORNING GLORY KEY
DMC stranded cotton
Cross stitch

		677
	676
	471
	989
	987
○	993
/	828
	827
□	813
•	blanc
■	310
M	5282 (gold metallic)

Backstitch
──── 310

BLUE MORNING GLORY

Heavenly blue morning glories climb skyward bringing their beauty with the first light of day.

In the cool of a summer morning they put on a showy display, closing their paper-thin petals to the afternoon

sun. A glittering dragonfly hovers nearby to take in their beauty.

DESIGN SIZE: 6 x 8cm (2⅜ x 3in)
STITCH COUNT: 43w x 57h

MATERIALS

• 13 x 18cm (5 x 7in) Rustico (#54) 18-count Aida
• DMC stranded cotton (floss) as listed in chart key
• Tapestry needle No.24

1 Begin by referring to Techniques, page 103 if necessary. Find and mark the centre of the fabric and circle the centre of the chart with a pen. Mount your fabric in an embroidery frame if you wish.

2 Begin stitching from the centre of your fabric, working outwards, following the colour changes on the chart. Work all the cross stitches using two strands of stranded cotton (floss). Work the black backstitch outlines using one strand.

3 Once all the stitching is complete, continue on to embroider the second flower design. Refer to page 108 for making up the designs into a wall hanging.

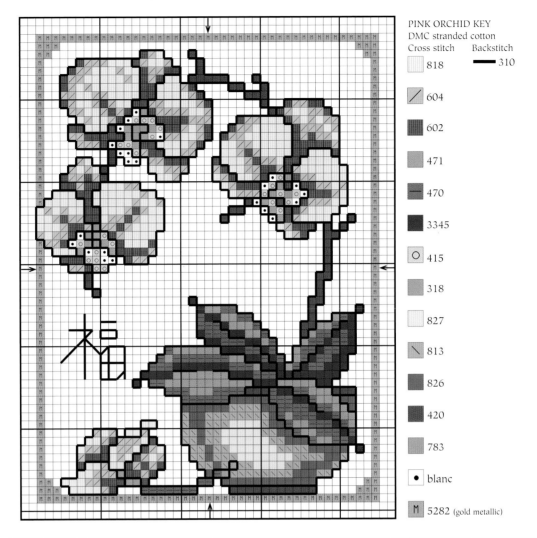

PINK ORCHID KEY
DMC stranded cotton
Cross stitch   Backstitch

818	——— 310
604	
602	
471	
470	
3345	
O 415	
318	
827	
813	
826	
420	
783	
• blanc	
M 5282 (gold metallic)	

PINK ORCHID

A prized orchid stem gracefully nods to show off its delicious pink blooms.

Evoking a sense of mystery and beauty, the flowers capture the imagination, while the

Chinese symbol for happiness completes the picture.

DESIGN SIZE: 6 x 8cm (2⅜ x 3in)
STITCH COUNT: 43w x 57h

MATERIALS
• 13 x 18cm (5 x 7in) Rustico (#54) 18-count Aida
• DMC stranded cotton (floss) as listed in the chart key
• Tapestry needle No.24

1 Begin by referring to Techniques page 103 if necessary. Find and mark the centre of the fabric and circle the centre of the chart with a pen. Mount your fabric in an embroidery frame if you wish.

2 Begin stitching from the centre of your fabric and work outwards, following the colour changes on the chart. Work all the cross stitches using two strands of stranded cotton (floss). Work the black backstitch outlines using one strand and the Chinese symbol outline with two strands.

3 Once all the stitching is complete, continue on to embroider the third flower design. Refer to page 108 for making up the designs into a wall hanging.

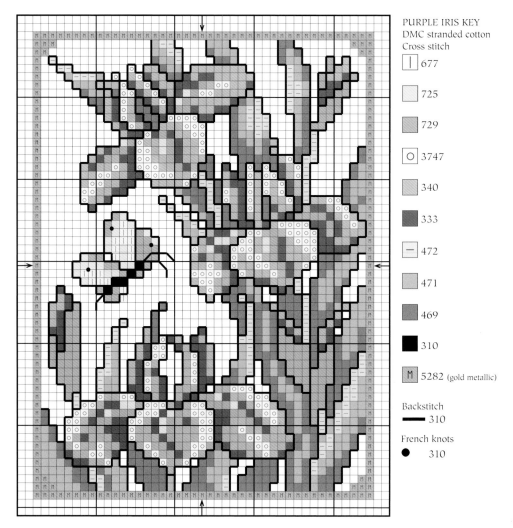

PURPLE IRIS KEY
DMC stranded cotton
Cross stitch

		677
	725
	729
O	3747
	340
	333
—	472
	471
	469
■	310
M	5282 (gold metallic)

Backstitch
—— 310

French knots
● 310

Purple Iris

In spring, the regal Siberian iris brings new life to the dormant garden, its velvet petals unfolding against a backdrop of tall leaves. In the practice of feng shui, it is said that these blue-green swords cut through stagnant ch'i bringing a smooth flow of positive energy to the garden.

DESIGN SIZE: 6 x 8cm (2⅜ x 3in)
STITCH COUNT: 43w x 57h

MATERIALS

- 13 x 18cm (5 x 7in) Rustico (#54) 18-count Aida
- DMC stranded cotton (floss) as listed in the chart key
- Tapestry needle No.24

1 Begin by referring to Techniques, page 103 if necessary. Find and mark the centre of the fabric and circle the centre of the chart with a pen. Mount your fabric in an embroidery frame if you wish.

2 Begin stitching from the centre of your fabric and work outwards, following the colour changes on the chart. Work the cross stitches using two strands of stranded cotton (floss) and the three black French knots on the butterfly wings also with two strands. Work the black backstitch outlines using one strand.

3 Once all the stitching is complete, make up the three designs into a wall hanging, as described on page 108.

Bird on Blossom

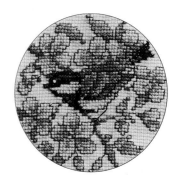

Season-to-season change moves through the garden: nature's transitions are in evidence everywhere. Sunshine plays through the leaves and branches of the trees, casting their shadows on the path below. Early-morning dew clings to the surface of velvet petals only to disappear in the growing light. The cycle of life ebbs and flows providing endless wonder for those partaking of the garden's mysteries.

Feng shui acknowledges the forces of the natural world and provides its practitioners with the means to coexist in tune with the world around them, bringing health, prosperity and happiness into their lives.

Springtime cherry blossoms open their sweet petals for only a few days and the fleeting beauty of their glorious display reminds us of our own place on this earth and how precious our time here is. With these thoughts comes the knowledge that the flowers bring the fruit of the tree and the fruit the seed of new life – the eternal cycle ever flowing.

A tiny black-bibbed chickadee is perched amongst the flowers. A visitor to the garden throughout the year, he brings a message of courage and hope. Even in the cold winters of my own garden I see him darting swiftly between the snow-covered branches, a constant presence in an ever-changing setting. The linens presented here will bring a touch of spring to your table. Chinese double happiness medallions containing the words 'one with heaven' bring a wish for inner peace and tranquillity of the heart.

BIRD ON BLOSSOM
TABLECLOTH

The tender blossoms of the cherry tree and sweetly chirping chickadee fill this beautiful damask tablecloth with the spirit of the springtime garden. Enjoy an afternoon cup of tea with a touch of nature and a wish for happiness.

DESIGN SIZE: 59.5 x 59.5cm (23½ x 23½in)
STITCH COUNT: 239w x 239h

MATERIALS

- 80cm (31½in) square Zweigart Largo table topper (#2453) in eggshell (#12) 11-count Aida
- DMC stranded cotton (floss) listed in the chart key
- Tapestry needle No.24

1 Begin by referring to Techniques page 103 if necessary. The design has two different bird and blossom motifs, to be stitched in opposite corners of the tablecloth. Refer to the whole tablecloth design diagram on page 60, with instructions on using the charts. You will find it helpful to enlarge the charts on a colour photocopier.

2 Work the cross stitches using two strands of stranded cotton (floss) and the backstitches using one strand. Note: the black backstitch is shown in dark grey on the charts for clarity.

3 Once all the stitching is complete, press the table-cloth carefully if required.

Classical Chinese painting often celebrated the beauty of nature and the changing seasons. These Bird on Blossom table linens are decorated with two enchanting symbols of spring and the stylized symbol for double happiness. These motifs can also be adapted to other pre-finished items such as placemats, table runners or even a delicate border on bed linens

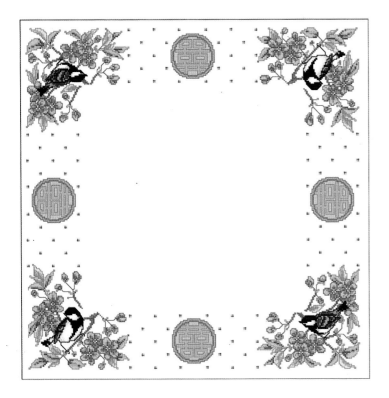

USING THE BIRD ON BLOSSOM CHARTS

The Tablecloth Because of the size of the table-cloth, only the repeated parts of the charts are given, with the whole tablecloth design shown left. Start by stitching the two parts of the chart provided below and on page 61, positioning them carefully within the lower border of your tablecloth. Then, counting carefully, turn the charts through 180° and stitch them again, this time within the top border of your tablecloth. The side borders can then be stitched using the relevant parts of the charts. (You may prefer to stitch the side borders before the top border to make counting easier.)

The Napkins The napkin charts on pages 62–3 show the two bird motifs, plus the corner border – refer to page 62 for the whole napkin design. Start by stitching the bird within the Aida circle in the corner of your napkin. Then stitch the little blossom clusters vertically and horizontally along the napkin borders, completing the corners by using the corner border chart turned through 90° each time.

BIRD ON BLOSSOM TABLECLOTH KEY
DMC stranded cotton
Cross stitch

/	729	O	369	• blanc
	680	ı	368	
\	869		367	**Backstitch**
	818	z	822	—— 310
□	776	X	644	—— 319
	899	I	318	—— 801
	472		317	**French knots**
△	471		413	O blanc
-	470	•	310	

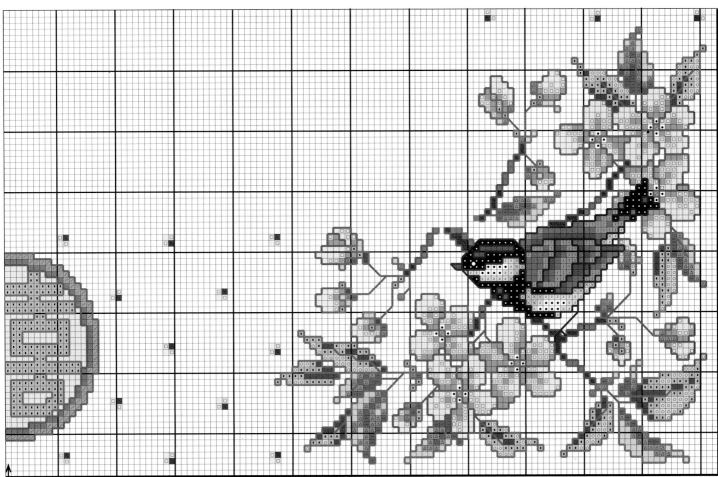

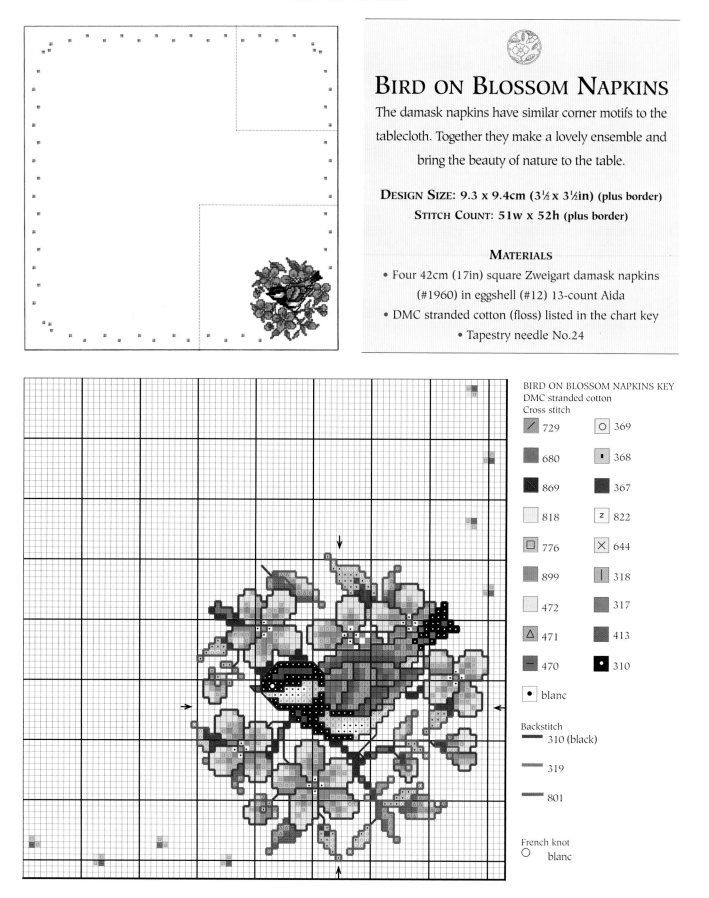

BIRD ON BLOSSOM NAPKINS

The damask napkins have similar corner motifs to the tablecloth. Together they make a lovely ensemble and bring the beauty of nature to the table.

DESIGN SIZE: 9.3 x 9.4cm (3½ x 3½in) (plus border)
STITCH COUNT: 51w x 52h (plus border)

MATERIALS

- Four 42cm (17in) square Zweigart damask napkins (#1960) in eggshell (#12) 13-count Aida
- DMC stranded cotton (floss) listed in the chart key
- Tapestry needle No.24

BIRD ON BLOSSOM NAPKINS KEY
DMC stranded cotton
Cross stitch

/	729	O	369
	680	·	368
X	869		367
	818	z	822
□	776	X	644
	899	I	318
	472		317
△	471		413
—	470	●	310
●	blanc		

Backstitch
— 310 (black)
— 319
— 801

French knot
O   blanc

1 Begin by referring to Techniques page 103 if necessary. There are two different bird and blossom motifs: two napkins feature one design and two napkins feature the other design. Refer to the instructions on page 60 for using the charts and take care to position the motif accurately within the Aida circle in the napkin each time.

2 Work the cross stitches using two strands of stranded cotton (floss) and the backstitches using one strand. The black backstitch is shown on the chart in dark grey for clarity. Work the cross stitch blossoms around the border to finish.

3 Once all the stitching is complete, press the napkins carefully if required.

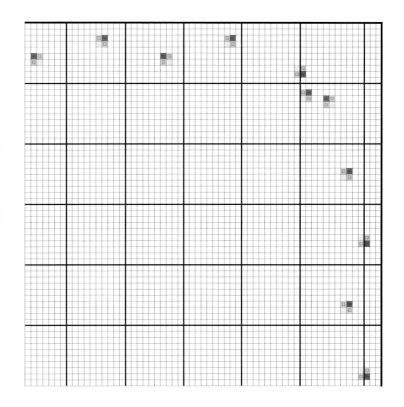

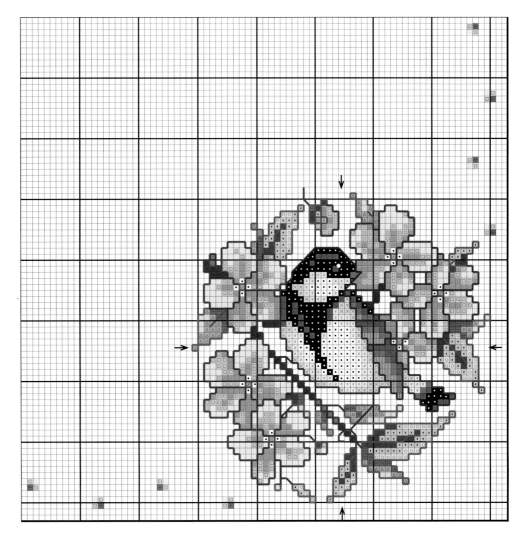

Chinese Flowers

Flowers enrich our lives with their delicious fragrance, luminous colours and diverse forms. The velvety petals of the iris speak softly of hope. Faith is restored as they raise their heads above blue-green leaves in the springtime garden. Standing tall and straight along the river's edge, the arching petals sway softly with the spring breezes. Their light, graceful form and deep-reaching roots are a testimony to the beauty and endurance of nature.

The voluptuous blooms of the peony have adorned tapestries, scroll paintings, fans and kimonos for centuries. The propagation of these plants involved painstaking care and attention and it became the favoured flower of the noble classes in China and Japan. As its reputation and culture grew, the regal peony with its abundance of flowers became a symbol of prosperity. It was said that in bud it acted as an aphrodisiac, the secret of which was held within its many layers of tightly clenched petals. The tree peony is one of the most glorious shrubs in the garden, the silken petals in colours of soft pink, deep red, creamy yellow and pristine white, dazzling those who pass by.

Ikebana, the traditional art of flower arrangement, dates from the sixth century in Japan when Buddhist priests presented flowers as offerings to Buddha. The three elements of heaven, earth and mankind are expressed in a balanced arrangement of natural flowers.

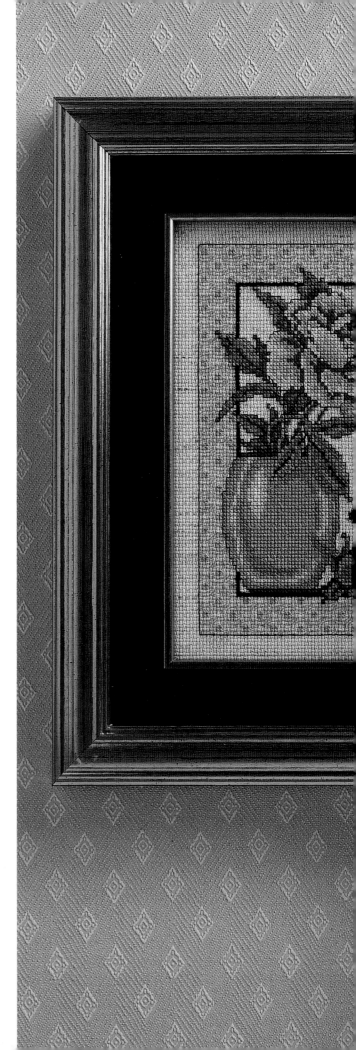

IRIS FLOWER OF BEAUTY

In this design, a glazed bowl the colour of rich earth holds three stately blue-violet Siberian irises. The graceful strokes of the Chinese symbol for beauty repeat the shape of the flowers. The moss green border, representing new life and healing, is an interpretation of the vintage silk brocades often used to mount flower paintings in China and Japan.

DESIGN SIZE: 15.25 x 20.3cm (6 x 8in)

STITCH COUNT: 84w x 112h

MATERIALS

- 28 x 33cm (11 x 13in) Rustico (#54) 14-count Aida
- DMC stranded cotton (floss) as listed in the chart key
- Tapestry needle No.24

1 Begin by referring to Techniques, page 103 if necessary. Find and mark the centre of the fabric and then circle the centre of the chart with a pen. Mount your fabric in an embroidery frame if you wish.

2 Begin stitching from the centre of your fabric and work outwards, following the colour changes on the chart. Work all the cross stitches using two strands of stranded cotton (floss). Refer to the chart key for working the various backstitches.

3 Once all the stitching is complete, finish your picture by mounting in a suitable frame (see page 106).

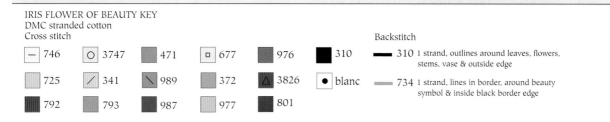

IRIS FLOWER OF BEAUTY KEY
DMC stranded cotton
Cross stitch

— 746	O 3747	471	□ 677	976	■ 310	• blanc
725	/ 341	\ 989	372	△ 3826		
792	793	987	977	801		

Backstitch

— 310 1 strand, outlines around leaves, flowers, stems, vase & outside edge

— 734 1 strand, lines in border, around beauty symbol & inside black border edge

PEONY FLOWER OF PEACE

A simple celadon vase holds one silky peony bloom, the grey-green leaves gracefully providing the perfect backdrop for the showy flower. The Chinese character for peace expresses the balance between opposing forces. As ikebana strives to create balance in colour and form, heaven and nature harmonize to create peace.

DESIGN SIZE: 15.25 x 20.3cm (6 x 8in)
STITCH COUNT: 84w x 112h

MATERIALS

• 28 x 33cm (11 x 13in) Rustico (#54) 14-count Aida
• DMC stranded cotton (floss) as listed
in the chart key
• Tapestry needle No.24

1 Begin by referring to Techniques, page 103 if necessary. Find and mark the centre of the fabric and then circle the centre of the chart with a pen. Mount your fabric in an embroidery frame if you wish.

2 Begin stitching from the centre of your fabric and work outwards, following the colour changes on the chart. Work all the cross stitches using two strands of stranded cotton (floss). Refer to the chart key for working the various backstitches.

3 Once all the stitching is complete, finish your picture by mounting in a suitable frame (see page 106).

PEONY FLOWER OF PEACE KEY
DMC stranded cotton
Cross stitch

					Backstitch	
725	502	3363	310	O 604	— 310	1 strand, outlines around leaves, flowers, stems, vase & outside edge
504	− 676	3051	/ 818	602	═ 729	1 strand, lines in border, around peace symbol & inside black border edge
△ 503	3364	975	605	• blanc		

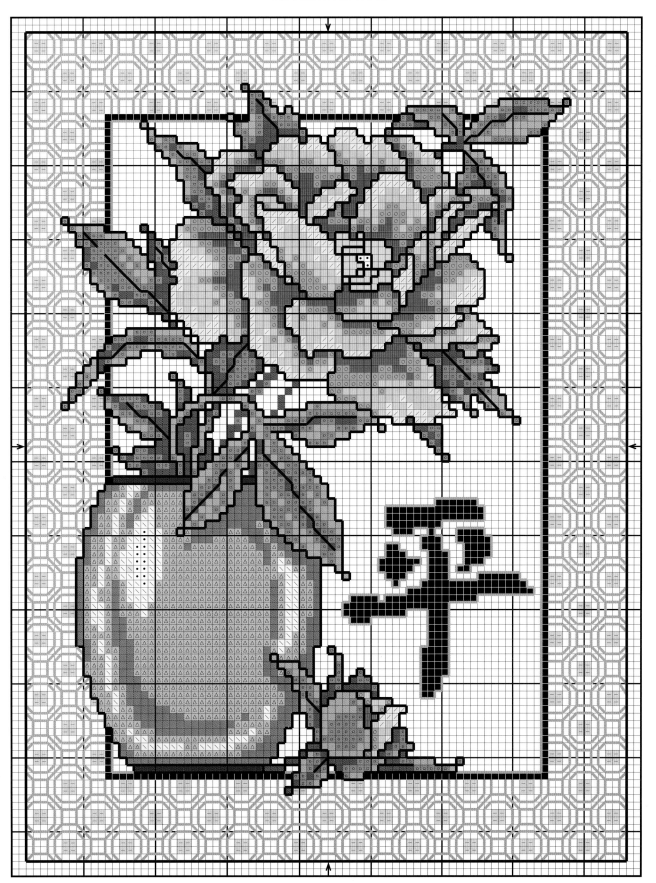

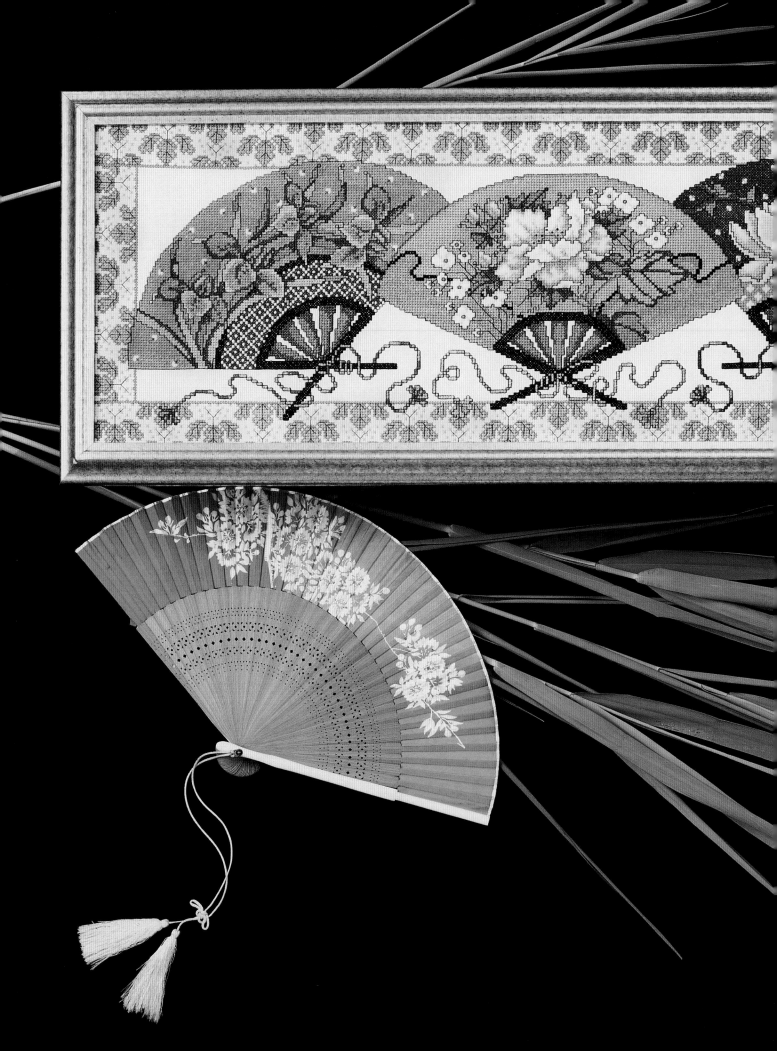

Fans of the Far East

For centuries, fans have played an important role in Chinese and Japanese culture and it is said that the folding fan appeared in Japan as early as the seventh century. Many different classes of fans were created, each with its own special purpose or ceremony. So much importance was placed on the fan that the decoration became a work of art in itself. These paintings were often done on silk or gilded paper with bird, flower or animal motifs, and the vivid renderings allowed the artist to bring nature indoors.

The three fans in this arrangement bring three different flowers into your home. The Siberian iris is the flower of faith and hope. The exquisite Japanese peony brings to mind opulence and luxury. The creamy-yellow magnolia represents tenderness and love of nature.

Evoking the luxurious silks of the Orient, rich colours, traditional geometric and wave patterns, and a flowing, silky tassel complete each fan. The border motif for this picture was inspired by the silk brocade used to mount traditional Chinese scroll paintings.

程 *Fans played an important role, being carried by both men and women. There were different classes of fans, each reserved for a special ceremony or use. Leading Chinese painters used the fan as a canvas for their finest work. Ethereal landscapes and vivid renditions of birds and flowers brought nature indoors.*

FANS OF THE FAR
EAST KEY
DMC stranded cotton
Cross stitch

818

/ 3326

899 (2 skeins)

\ 341

340

333

- 799

311 (2 skeins)

677

729 (2 skeins)

z 680

l 435

433

3053

503 (3 skeins)

502 (2 skeins)

936 (2 skeins)

453

452

310 (3 skeins)

• blanc

Backstitch

936

310

French knots

● 310

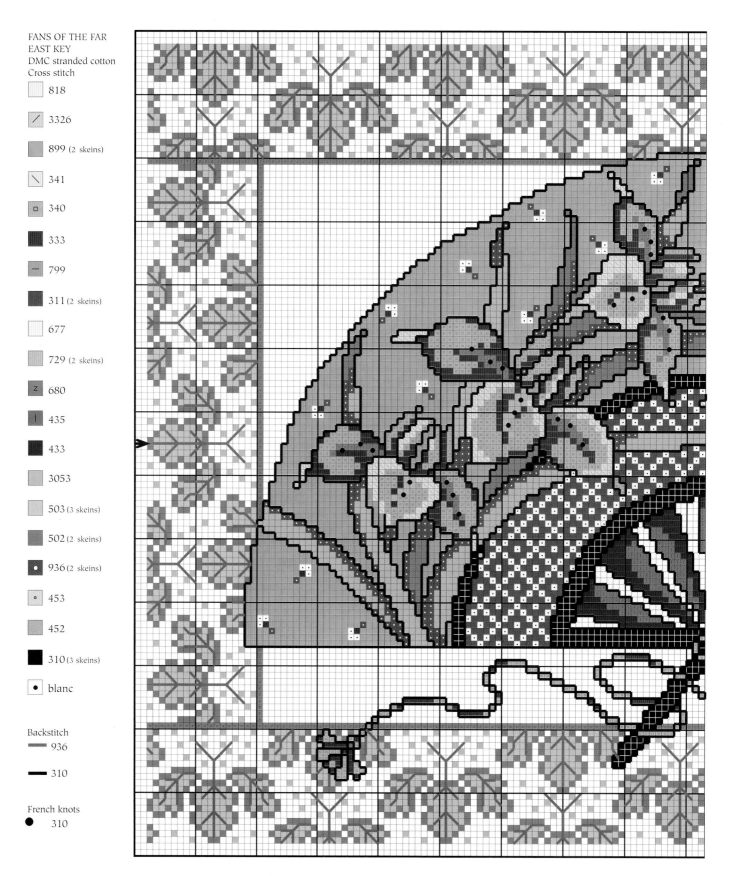

FANS OF THE
FAR EAST KEY
DMC stranded cotton
Cross stitch

818
3326
899 (2 skeins)
341
340
333
799
311 (2 skeins)
677
729 (2 skeins)
680
435
433
3053
503 (3 skeins)
502 (2 skeins)
936 (2 skeins)
453
452
310 (3 skeins)
blanc

Backstitch
936
310

French knots
310

DESIGN SIZE: 66 x 22.8cm (26 x 9in)
STITCH COUNT: 364w x 126h

MATERIALS
- 76 x 33cm (30 x 13in) white 14-count Aida
- DMC stranded cotton (floss) as listed in the chart key
- Tapestry needle No.24

1 Begin by referring to Techniques, page 103, if necessary. Find and mark the centre of the fabric and then circle the centre of the chart with a pen. Mount your fabric in an embroidery frame if you wish.

2 Begin stitching from the centre of your fabric and work outwards, following the colour changes on the chart. Note: some colours use more than one skein. Work all the cross stitches and the black French knots using two strands of stranded cotton (floss) and the backstitch outlining using one strand.

3 Once all the stitching is complete, finish your picture by mounting in a suitable frame (see page 106 for advice).

Oriental Greetings

This collection of four greeting cards features a Chinese symbol on each design to express a special sentiment to friends and loved ones.

The character for longevity represents the spirit of a life well lived. Plum blossoms, the flower of long life and endurance, grace the border and are said to grow more beautiful every year the tree ages.

The spiritual meaning of the symbol for prosperity is the fullness of a life blessed with the riches of the heart such as love, generosity and inner peace. The tiny, pink buds of spring jasmine adorn the border of this card, a sign of good luck and prosperity.

The kanji symbol for benevolence represents two people and the spirit of doing good towards others. A border of irises frames this simple figure, the purple flowers sending a message of friendship and appreciation.

The character for love represents the spirit that brings life to the heart and grace to the soul. Clear blue morning glories fill the border in a tender expression of affection.

Chinese kanji characters express their meaning through analogy with nature, at times using several different images to make up one word. For example, the kanji for gentleness combines the symbols for leaf and stream. An image of a small leaf carried effortlessly on the current of a quiet stream captures the Tao spirit of gentleness. Love, considered a highly spiritual emotion, is a combination of three symbols that represent the heart surrounded by beauty and graceful movement.

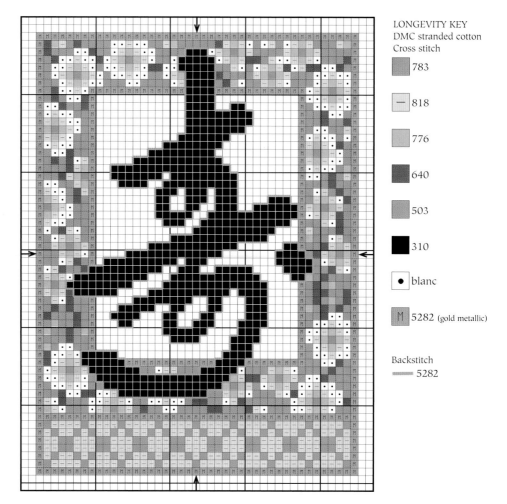

LONGEVITY KEY
DMC stranded cotton
Cross stitch

	783
–	818
	776
	640
	503
	310
•	blanc
M	5282 (gold metallic)

Backstitch
━━━ 5282

LONGEVITY

The graceful flow of the brush strokes in this character carry the spirit of life's energy on its eternal path.

This card with its enduring message of long life works well as a birthday wish or as a loving sentiment

for a special couple on their anniversary.

DESIGN SIZE: 6 x 8cm (2⅜ x 3in)
STITCH COUNT: 43w x 57h

MATERIALS

• 13 x 18cm (5 x 7in) Rustico (#54) 18-count Aida
• DMC stranded cotton (floss) as listed in the chart key
• Tapestry needle No.24

1 Begin by referring to Techniques page 103 if necessary. Find and mark the centre of the fabric and circle the centre of the chart with a pen. Mount your fabric in an embroidery frame if you wish.

2 Begin stitching from the centre of your fabric and work outwards, following the colour changes on the chart. Work all the cross stitches using two strands of stranded cotton (floss) and the 5282 (gold metallic) backstitch outlines using two strands.

3 Once all the stitching is complete, mount your embroidery in a suitable card (see page 106). See page 106 also for suggestions on decorating card mounts.

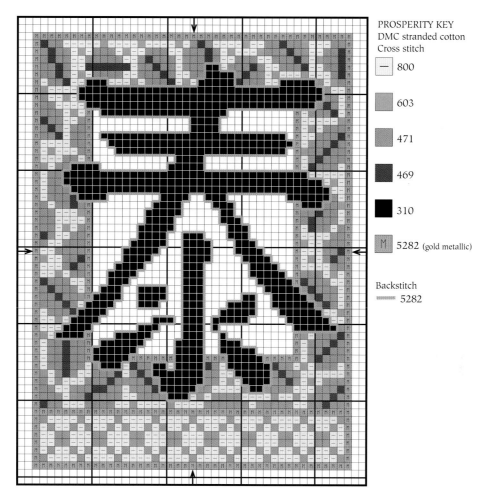

PROSPERITY KEY
DMC stranded cotton
Cross stitch

- — 800
- 603
- 471
- 469
- 310
- M 5282 (gold metallic)

Backstitch
5282

PROSPERITY

A rich life begins with spiritual wealth. Whether recognising a unique personal accomplishment or an exciting new endeavour, this symbol will deliver your heartfelt message of prosperity and good luck to someone special.

DESIGN SIZE: 6 x 8cm (2⅜ x 3in)
STITCH COUNT: 43w x 57h

MATERIALS

- 13 x 18cm (5 x 7in) Rustico (#54) 18-count Aida
- DMC stranded cotton (floss) as listed in the chart key
- Tapestry needle No.24

1 Begin by referring to Techniques page 103 if necessary. Find and mark the centre of the fabric and circle the centre of the chart with a pen. Mount your fabric in an embroidery frame if you wish.

2 Begin stitching from the centre of your fabric and work outwards, following the colour changes on the chart. Work all the cross stitches using two strands of stranded cotton (floss) and the 5282 (gold metallic) backstitch outlines using two strands.

3 Once all the stitching is complete, mount your embroidery in a suitable card (see page 106). See page 106 also for suggestions on decorating card mounts.

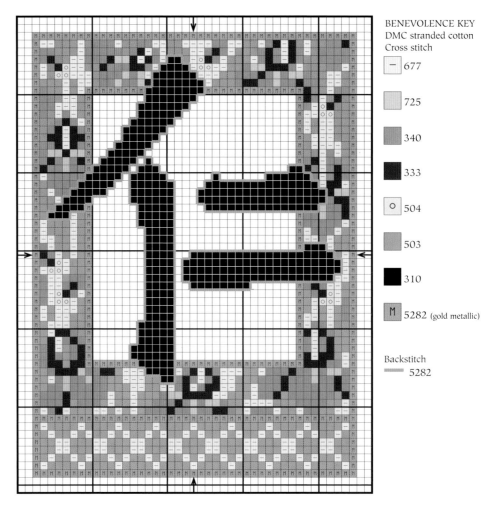

BENEVOLENCE KEY
DMC stranded cotton
Cross stitch

−	677
	725
	340
	333
○	504
	503
	310
M	5282 (gold metallic)

Backstitch
▬▬▬ 5282

BENEVOLENCE

Confucius considered kindness and humanity to be the first of the Four Virtues. Sharing our spirit can bring joy and comfort to those around us. Send this symbol of caring as an expression of appreciation to someone who has shown you a special kindness at just the right moment.

DESIGN SIZE: 6 x 8cm (2⅜ x 3in)
STITCH COUNT: 43w x 57h

MATERIALS

• 13 x 18cm (5 x 7in) Rustico (#54) 18-count Aida
• DMC stranded cotton (floss) as listed in the chart key
• Tapestry needle No.24

1 Begin by referring to Techniques page 103 if necessary. Find and mark the centre of the fabric and circle the centre of the chart with a pen. Mount your fabric in an embroidery frame if you wish.

2 Begin stitching from the centre of your fabric and work outwards, following the colour changes on the chart. Work all the cross stitches using two strands of stranded cotton (floss) and the 5282 (gold metallic) backstitch outlines using two strands.

3 Once all the stitching is complete, mount your embroidery in a suitable card (see page 106). See page 106 also for suggestions on decorating card mounts.

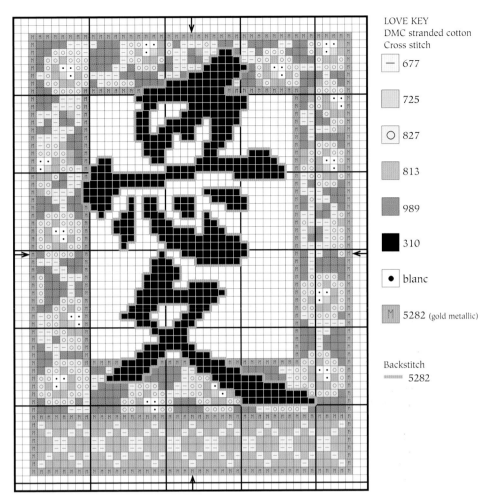

LOVE KEY
DMC stranded cotton
Cross stitch

—	677
░	725
O	827
▨	813
▨	989
■	310
•	blanc
M	5282 (gold metallic)

Backstitch
▭▭▭ 5282

LOVE

The spirit of love is elegantly expressed in the brush strokes of this character. This card is the perfect
messenger for sending a comforting note, to tell someone away from home that they are in your thoughts,
or just to say I love you.

DESIGN SIZE: 6 x 8cm (2⅜ x 3in)
STITCH COUNT: 43w x 57h

MATERIALS
- 13 x 18cm (5 x 7in) Rustico (#54) 18-count Aida
- DMC stranded cotton (floss) as listed in the chart key
- Tapestry needle No.24

1 Begin by referring to Techniques page 103 if necessary.
Find and mark the centre of the fabric and circle the
centre of the chart with a pen. Mount your fabric in an
embroidery frame if you wish.

2 Begin stitching from the centre of your fabric and work
outwards, following the colour changes on the chart.
Work all the cross stitches using two strands of stranded
cotton (floss) and the 5282 (gold metallic) backstitch outlines using two strands.

3 Once all the stitching is complete, mount your embroidery in a suitable card (see page 106). See page 106
also for suggestions on decorating card mounts.

Oriental Lady Wisdom

In this picture the earthy sienna brown, rich gold and sensuous red of the autumn landscape colour the enveloping layers of kimono worn by the figure of Wisdom. The artists of Edo Period Japan were able to capture the essence of a beautiful woman in a simple gesture of the hand or a turn of the head. This design draws on that perfect clarity of movement.

Today the kimono is worn for special ceremonies and occasions but during the Edo period of Japan it was the ultimate symbol of affluence, to be worn and displayed whenever possible. It was at this time that the kimono became art as fashion.

The eternal circle of heaven holds an autumn sky fading to twilight, the perfect backdrop for the brilliant red leaves of the Japanese maple. Autumn is a time of abundance and harvest, when the earth releases her precious gifts. The open fan displays the intense gold and reds of the setting sun while the cool colours of the sea carry the spirit of life. Radiant, silk-embroidered chrysanthemums, symbolizing friendship, contentment and the light of hope, dance across the outer layer of the kimono. The intricately tied obi is sewn from regal golden silk, embellished with roundels of stylized red chrysanthemums. The soft colours of the inner robes repeat the poetry of the changing season, each layer chosen to complement the other. In a grand gesture, Wisdom releases her knowledge, reminding us that the beauty of life lies in its never-ending cycle of change and renewal.

DESIGN SIZE: 33 x 42.5cm (13 x 16¾in)
STITCH COUNT: 184w x 236h

MATERIALS
• 46 x 56cm (18 x 22in) Rustico (#54) 14-count Aida
• DMC stranded cotton (floss) as listed in the chart key
• Tapestry needle No.24

1 Begin by referring to Techniques, page 103, if necessary. Find and mark the centre of the Aida fabric and then circle the centre of the chart with a pen. Mount your fabric in an embroidery frame if you wish.

2 Begin stitching from the centre of your fabric and work outwards, following the colour changes on the chart. Note: some colours use more than one skein. Work the cross stitches using two strands of stranded cotton (floss). Refer to the chart key for working all the backstitches.

3 Once all the stitching is complete, finish your picture by mounting in a suitable frame (see page 106).

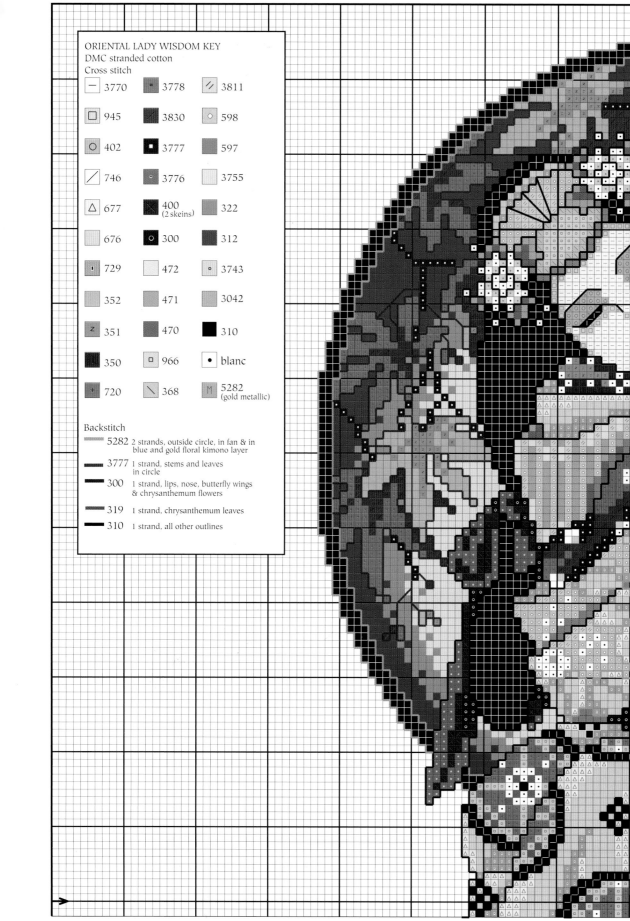

ORIENTAL LADY WISDOM KEY
DMC stranded cotton
Cross stitch

— 3770	3778	3811
945	3830	○ 598
○ 402	3777	597
/ 746	3776	3755
△ 677	400 (2 skeins)	322
676	○ 300	312
729	472	3743
352	471	3042
z 351	470	310
350	966	• blanc
+ 720	368	M 5282 (gold metallic)

Backstitch

5282 2 strands, outside circle, in fan & in blue and gold floral kimono layer

3777 1 strand, stems and leaves in circle

300 1 strand, lips, nose, butterfly wings & chrysanthemum flowers

319 1 strand, chrysanthemum leaves

310 1 strand, all other outlines

84

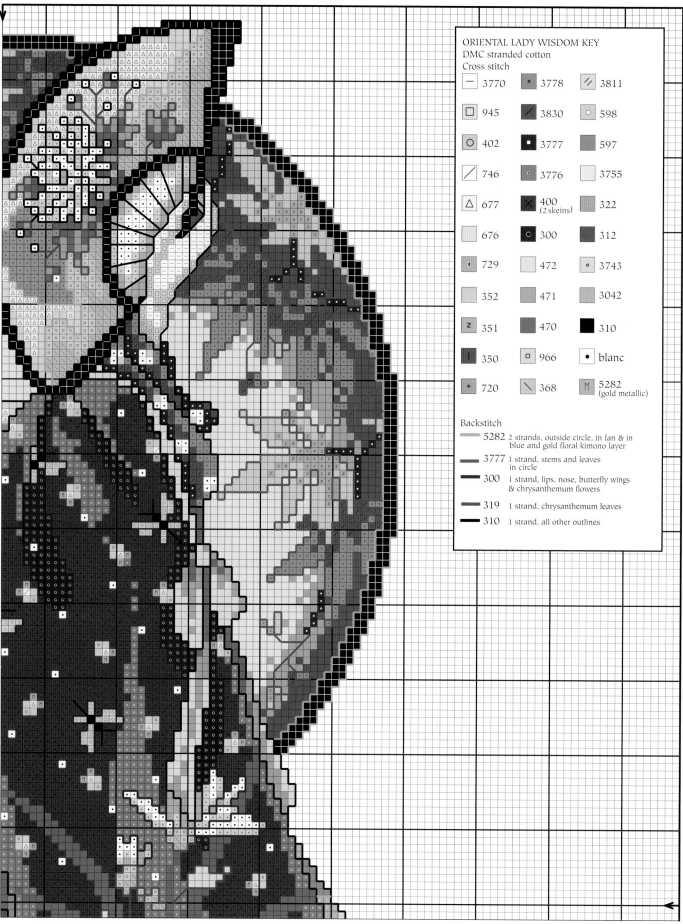

ORIENTAL LADY WISDOM KEY
DMC stranded cotton
Cross stitch

–	3770		3778		3811
□	945		3830	○	598
○	402		3777		597
/	746		3776		3755
△	677	✕	400 (2 skeins)		322
	676	○	300		312
•	729		472		3743
	352		471		3042
z	351		470	■	310
	350	□	966	•	blanc
+	720	\	368	M	5282 (gold metallic)

Backstitch

5282 2 strands, outside circle, in fan & in blue and gold floral kimono layer

3777 1 strand, stems and leaves in circle

300 1 strand, lips, nose, butterfly wings & chrysanthemum flowers

319 1 strand, chrysanthemum leaves

310 1 strand, all other outlines

Triptych Pillow

A symbol of prosperity and an expression of style, kimonos were sewn in luxurious silks and intricately hand-painted, embroidered and tie-dyed. The painted fans of both China and Japan bore the same purpose. Created to suit the particular occasion, they were carried by both men and women and became an important accessory. While depicting the beauty of nature and reflecting the personality of the owner, they also served as a subtle guise for seduction.

The two fans in this design reflect the glory of the spring garden, their traditional round shape representing the spirit of heaven. On the left, fragrant peach blossoms open their soft petals to the sky. The fragile blooms are a symbol of long life and hold the promise of the future. On the right, hanging clusters of wisteria, the flower of gentleness and invitation, grace the sky-blue background of the second fan, promising a life of ease and contentment. Centred on the pillow is a striking silk kimono of deep midnight blue, the colour of knowledge and understanding. Pink peonies, a flower of nobility, honour and abundance are gathered in a gilded bundle.

The expansion of popular culture in eighteenth and nineteenth century Japan allowed the urban merchant classes access to art and design previously reserved for the higher nobility. Artists used the fan and the kimono as blank canvases on which to display some of their most accomplished work.

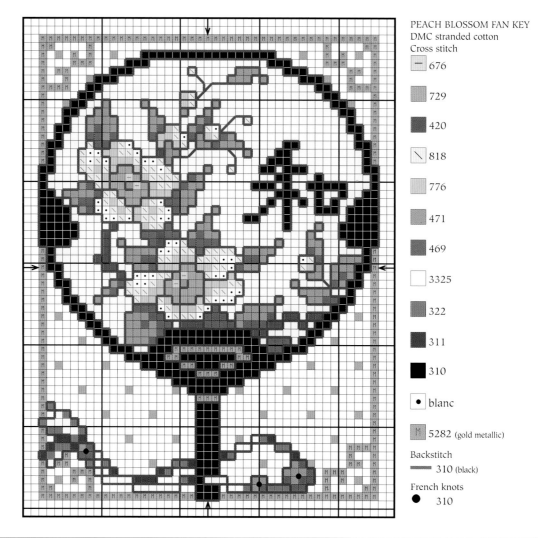

PEACH BLOSSOM FAN KEY
DMC stranded cotton
Cross stitch

—	676
	729
	420
\	818
	776
	471
	469
	3325
	322
	311
	310
•	blanc
M	5282 (gold metallic)

Backstitch
—— 310 (black)

French knots
● 310

PEACH BLOSSOM FAN

Poetic lines were often used on fans as part of the overall design. The kanji symbol for harmony on this fan shows the oneness of nature. It is the intertwining forces of nature that create the eternal cycle of life, allowing the peach tree to re-awaken every spring.

DESIGN SIZE: 6 x 8cm (2³⁄₁₆ x 3¹⁄₁₆in)
STITCH COUNT: 43w x 57h

MATERIALS

• 13 x 18cm (5 x 7in) Rustico (#54) 18-count Aida
• DMC stranded cotton (floss) as listed in the chart key
• Tapestry needle No.24

1 Refer to Techniques page 103 if necessary. Find and mark the centre of the fabric and circle the centre of the chart. Use an embroidery frame if you wish.

2 Begin stitching from the fabric centre and work outwards, following the colour changes on the chart. Work the cross stitches using two strands of stranded cotton (floss) and the French knots with two strands of black wound once around the needle. Using one strand, work the black backstitch outlines (shown in dark grey on the chart for clarity).

3 Once all the stitching is complete, continue on to embroider the second triptych design. Refer to page 107 for making up the designs into a pillow.

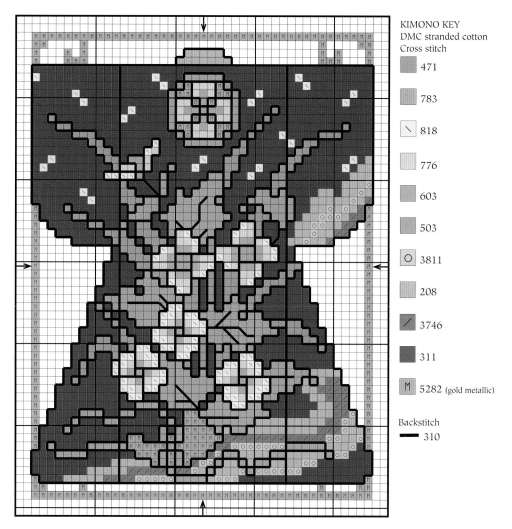

KIMONO KEY
DMC stranded cotton
Cross stitch

▨	471
▨	783
＼	818
▨	776
▨	603
▨	503
○	3811
▨	208
╱	3746
▨	311
M	5282 (gold metallic)

Backstitch
— 310

KIMONO

Today, vintage kimonos are displayed as treasured works of art. Embroidered with the classic flowers of the Orient, this opulent garment is hung on a gilded frame, the sides unfolded to show the flowing movement of nature.

DESIGN SIZE: 6 x 8cm (2³⁄₁₆ x 3¹⁄₁₆in)
STITCH COUNT: 43w x 57h

MATERIALS
- 13 x 18cm (5 x 7in) Rustico (#54) 18-count Aida
- DMC stranded cotton (floss) as listed in the chart key
- Tapestry needle No.24

1 Begin by referring to Techniques page 103 if necessary. Find and mark the centre of the Aida fabric and circle the centre of the chart with a pen. Mount your fabric in an embroidery frame if you wish.

2 Begin stitching from the centre of your fabric and work outwards, following the colour changes on the chart. Work all the cross stitches using two strands of stranded cotton (floss). Work the black backstitch outlines using one strand.

3 Once all the stitching is complete, continue on to embroider the third triptych design. Refer to page 107 for making up the designs into a pillow.

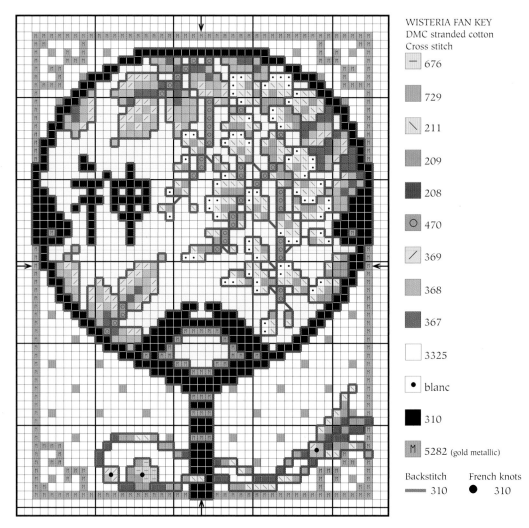

WISTERIA FAN KEY
DMC stranded cotton
Cross stitch

—	676
	729
\	211
	209
	208
○	470
/	369
	368
	367
	3325
•	blanc
	310
M	5282 (gold metallic)

Backstitch	French knots
—— 310	● 310

WISTERIA FAN

Calligraphers often used fans as a canvas for their expressive brush strokes. The symbol for spirit represents the essential energy of life. Every living thing shares this spirit, just as the wisteria offers its sweet flowers of gentle invitation to all who pass by.

DESIGN SIZE: 6 x 8cm (2³⁄₁₆ x 3¹⁄₁₆in)
STITCH COUNT: 43w x 57h

MATERIALS
• 13 x 18cm (5 x 7in) Rustico (#54) 18-count Aida
• DMC stranded cotton (floss) as listed in the chart key
• Tapestry needle No.24

1 Begin by referring to Techniques page 103 if necessary. Find and mark the centre of the Aida fabric and circle the centre of the chart with a pen. Mount your fabric in an embroidery frame if you wish.

2 Begin stitching from the centre of your fabric and work outwards, following the colour changes on the chart. Work all the cross stitches and the black French knots in the flower centres with two strands of stranded cotton (floss). Using one strand, work the black backstitch outlines (shown in dark grey on the chart for clarity).

3 Once all the stitching is complete, take the three designs and make up into a pillow as described on page 107.

Koi and Dragonflies

In shimmering patterns of colour, koi skim the surface of a pond and then suddenly retreat. Vibrant orange, black onyx and snow white paint the cool green water with light, the glistening shapes representing the free movement of the life force. Another gem of the water garden is the dragonfly. Hovering above the water, it glides past in a delicate dance, its gossamer wings glittering in the sunlight. Catching our hearts with its beauty, the dragonfly is a symbol of immortality and regeneration. It is nature's representative of the positive, free-flowing, eternal energy we all seek in our environment.

Koi are members of the carp family. Their full name in Japanese is nishikigoi, meaning living jewels. Bred for their pattern and colour, champion koi are highly prized treasures to collectors. They are a symbol of strength and sound judgement. On May 5, Children's Day in Japan, colourful fish banners are flown from doorways to bring strength and courage for the children of the household.

The colours of the koi and dragonfly are a perfect complement to one another. Red and orange are the colours of radiance and excitement, while blue is the colour of contemplation and peace. This combination illustrates the idea of opposing energies creating perfect harmony as in the t'ai ch'i symbol of yin and yang. Behind the motifs on these two towel borders, a quiet stream flows to carry the uninterrupted passage of ch'i to your home.

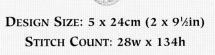

DESIGN SIZE: 5 x 24cm (2 x 9½in)
STITCH COUNT: 28w x 134h

MATERIALS
- Charles Craft fingertip towel (#VT 6900-2742) in ecru with 14-count insert (see Suppliers)
- DMC stranded cotton (floss) as listed in the chart key
- Tapestry needle No.24

1 Begin by referring to Techniques page 103 if necessary. Find and mark the centre of the towel band and then circle the centre of the chart with a pen.

2 Begin stitching from the centre of the band and work outwards, following the colour changes on the chart.

For the Koi Border: Work the cross stitches and the French knots with two strands of stranded cotton (floss) and the backstitch outlines with one strand of black to finish.

For the Dragonfly Border: Work the cross stitches with two strands of stranded cotton (floss) and the blue and black backstitches with one strand.

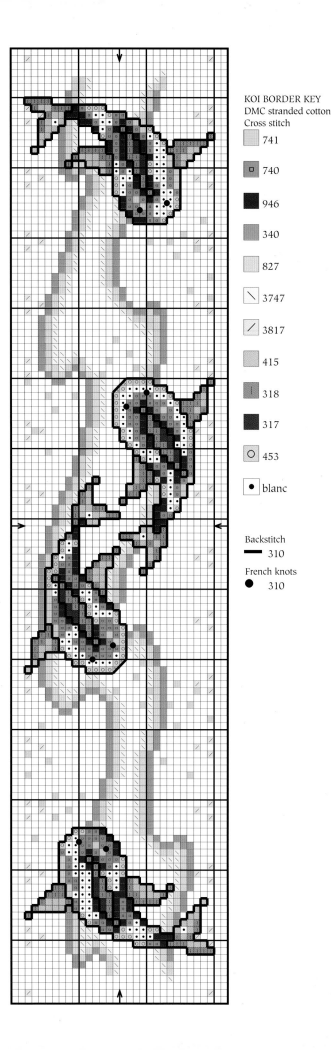

KOI BORDER KEY
DMC stranded cotton
Cross stitch

	741
□	740
■	946
	340
	827
\	3747
/	3817
	415
I	318
■	317
○	453
●	blanc

Backstitch
—— 310

French knots
● 310

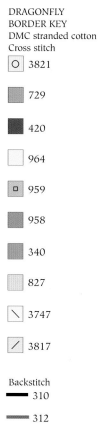

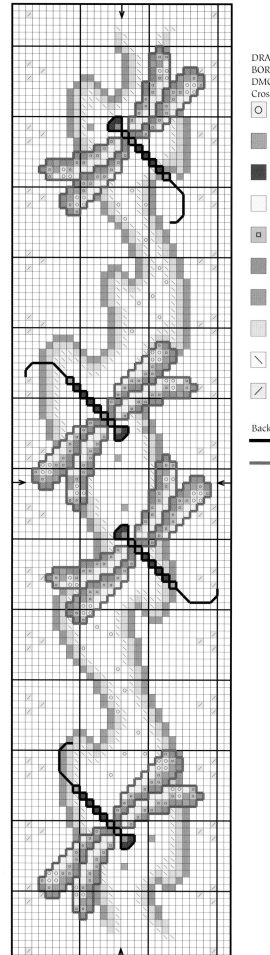

DRAGONFLY
BORDER KEY
DMC stranded cotton
Cross stitch

○	3821
	729
■	420
	964
□	959
	958
	340
	827
\	3747
/	3817

Backstitch
—— 310
—— 312

Harmony and Tranquillity

The flowers of exotic orchids lure us with their sensuous petals and beguiling scent. The diverse species of this mysterious plant have been a symbol of luxury, love and beauty for thousands of years. Noted in the writing of the Chinese philosopher Confucius, they are considered one of the Four Noble Plants of China, their exquisite form conveying the joy of friendship and a spirit of sincerity.

Chinese calligraphy is an art form used for thousands of years to express the essence of the human spirit through analogy with nature. Students of the calligrapher's art faithfully practise seven brushstrokes known as the Seven Mysteries. Mastery is reached when the character for eternity can be skilfully written, for it contains all of the Seven Mysteries.

In the ancient practice of feng shui, complementary forces of nature work as one to achieve a harmonious environment. The voluptuous blooms of the moth orchid bow gracefully to the Chinese characters for harmony and tranquillity, the refined brushstrokes leading the eye gently back to a single bloom carefully placed in a simple earthen bowl.

The pure white of the orchid alludes to the qualities of grace and enlightenment. The delicate inner petals are the pink colour of nourishment and hold the seductive nectar that sweetens the evening air. The arching stem springs from bold, rounded leaves the colour of new life and peace. Potted in a traditional celadon bowl, they create an elegant picture of aesthetic beauty. Leaves of golden bamboo frame the design, their gentle movement carefully balancing the tranquil message of the enchanting orchid.

DESIGN SIZE: 28 x 35.5cm (11 x 14in)
STITCH COUNT: 154w x 196h

MATERIALS
- 38 x 46cm (11 x 14in) Rustico (#54) 14-count Aida
- DMC stranded cotton (floss) as listed in the chart key
- Tapestry needle No.24

1 Begin by referring to Techniques page 103 if necessary. Find and mark the centre of the fabric and then circle the centre of the chart with a pen. Mount your fabric in an embroidery frame if you wish.

2 Begin stitching from the centre of your fabric and work outwards, following the colour changes on the chart. Note: some colours use more than one skein. Work all the cross stitches using two strands of stranded cotton (floss) and the backstitching and outlining using one strand of 938 (dark brown).

3 Once all the stitching is complete, finish your picture by mounting the embroidery in a suitable frame (see page 106 for advice).

HARMONY AND TRANQUILLITY KEY
DMC stranded cotton
Cross stitch

— 677	604	471	✕ 502	3345	434	│ 318	• blanc (2 skeins)
✕ 372 (2 skeins)	∘ 603	989	△ 503	╱ 436	680	317	
3011	601	▫ 987	504	● 801	415	■ 310 (2 skeins)	

Backstitch
—— 938

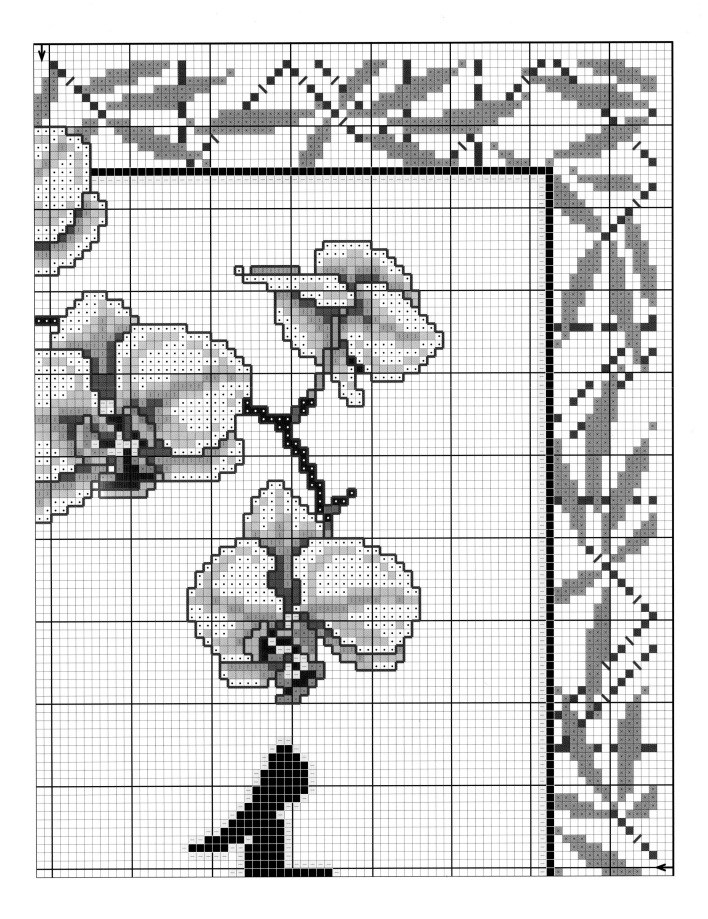

HARMONY AND TRANQUILLITY KEY
DMC stranded cotton
Cross stitch

— 677	604	471	502	3345	434	I 318	• blanc (2 skeins)
× 372 (2 skeins)	603	989	△ 503	436	680	317	
3011	601	987	504	801	415	310 (2 skeins)	Backstitch 938

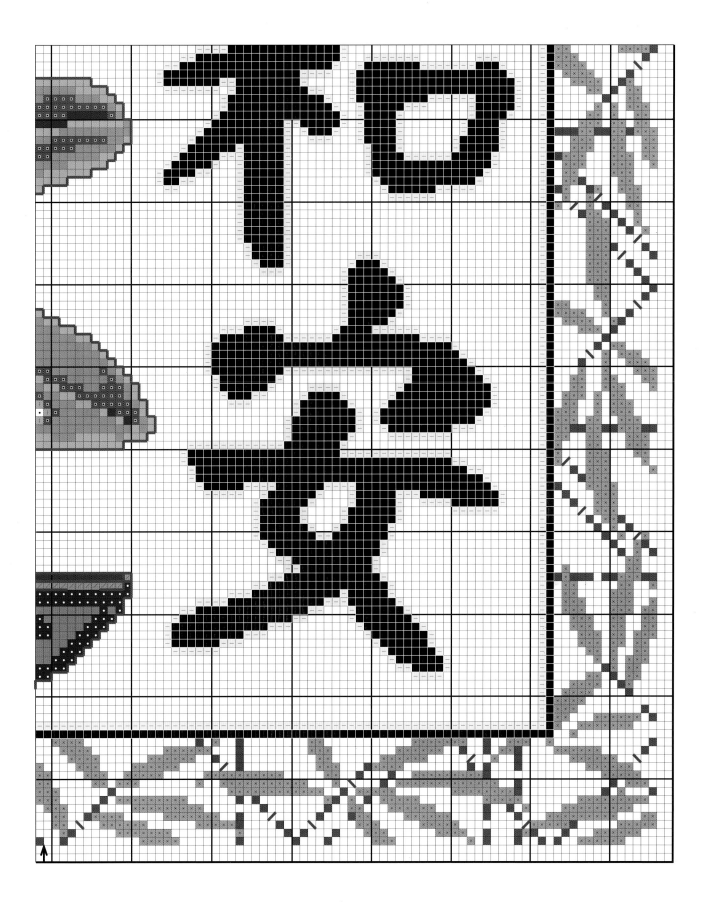

MATERIALS AND EQUIPMENT

The materials and equipment required for cross stitch embroidery are very simple and inexpensive, and this section describes the basics you will need. Refer to Suppliers for useful addresses.

FABRIC

The designs in this book have been worked predominantly on a blockweave fabric called Aida, where the stitches are worked into the holes in the fabric. If you change the gauge of the material, that is the number of holes per inch, then the size of the finished work will alter accordingly. The designs could also be stitched on an evenweave such as linen if you prefer, but if you do this remember to work over two fabric threads instead of one block.

THREADS

The projects have been stitched with DMC stranded embroidery cotton (floss) but conversion tables are available from the major thread manufacturers which give equivalent Anchor and Madeira stranded cotton (floss) colour codes if you prefer to use these, although exact colour matches are not always possible (see Suppliers).

The skeins of stranded cotton (floss) consist of six strands and can easily be split into separate threads. Each of the project instructions and chart keys will tell you how many strands to use. The chart keys assume that one skein of each colour will be needed, unless otherwise stated. It is a good idea to put the threads for a project on a sorter card or organiser.

NEEDLES

Tapestry needles are usually used for cross stitch as they have a rounded point and do not snag the material you are working with. They come in many different sizes and it is a matter of preference which size you use as long as the eye is big enough to accommodate the threads of embroidery cotton (floss) easily.

SCISSORS

Sharp, fine-pointed embroidery scissors will be needed for cutting threads, and a pair of dressmaking scissors for cutting fabric.

NEEDLEWORK FRAMES

Whether you use a wooden frame to keep your fabric taut while stitching is a matter of personal preference. Generally speaking, working with a frame helps to keep the tension even and prevent distortion, while working without a frame is faster and less cumbersome. There are various types on the market, so look in your local needlework shop.

TECHNIQUES

Cross stitch embroidery requires few complicated techniques but your stitching will look its best if you follow the simple guidelines described below. The projects in the book have been made up in various ways, described in Making Up Your Work beginning on page 105.

PREPARING THE FABRIC

Before starting, check carefully the Design Size given at the beginning of each project and make sure that this tallies with the size that you require for your finished embroidery. Then you should make sure that your fabric is at least 5cm (2in) larger all the way round than the finished size of the stitching, as this allows for making up. Before beginning to stitch, it is a good idea to neaten the edges of the fabric either by hemming or zig-zagging to stop the fabric fraying as you work.

MARKING THE CENTRE OF THE FABRIC

Regardless of which direction you work the design from it is important to find the centre point of the fabric in order to place the work centrally on the fabric. To find the centre, fold the fabric in half horizontally and then vertically, then tack (baste) along the folds. The centre point is where the two lines of tacking (basting) meet. Alternatively, you could use tailor's chalk to mark the lines. This point on the fabric corresponds to the centre point on the chart. Remove these tacked or chalk-marked lines on completion of the work.

USING THE CHARTS AND KEYS

The charts in this book are extremely clear to work from as they include symbols as well as colour blocks. Each square on the chart represents one stitch. Each coloured square/symbol represents a corresponding colour thread, given in the chart key. A few of the designs use fractional stitches (three-quarter and half

cross stitches) to give more definition. These are shown by half a square (a triangle) or a quarter square. Solid coloured lines show where backstitches are to be worked. French knots are shown by a coloured circle.

Each complete chart has black arrows at the sides to help you find the centre point easily. You may find it helpful to mark the centre point with a pen. Where the charts have been split over several pages, the chart key is repeated on each double page. You may find it useful to enlarge and colour photocopy the charts and tape the parts together. Numbering every tenth grid line (the darker lines) is also a good idea as it will make counting easier.

WASHING AND IRONING EMBROIDERY

If you find it necessary to wash embroidery, first make sure it is colourfast (particularly if you have used strong reds and blues), then wash with a gentle cleanser in tepid water. Squeeze gently but don't rub or wring. Rinse in plenty of cold or tepid water and allow to dry naturally.

To iron your work, use a medium setting and cover the ironing board with a thick layer of towelling. Place your stitching on this, right side down and press the embroidery gently to avoid flattening the stitches.

STARTING AND FINISHING STITCHING

Avoid using knots when starting and finishing as this will make your work lumpy when it is mounted. Instead, bring the needle up at the start of the first stitch, leaving a 'tail' of about 2.5cm (1in) at the back of your work. Secure the tail in place by working the first few stitches over it. Start new threads by first passing the needle through several stitches on the back of the work.

To finish off thread, pass the needle through some nearby stitches on the wrong side of the work, then cut the thread off, close to the fabric.

WORKING THE STITCHES

The designs are predominantly stitched with whole cross stitches though a few of the designs (the Oriental Ladies and Bird on Blossom) also use some fractional stitches for extra detail. The other stitches used are backstitches and French knots.

Backstitch

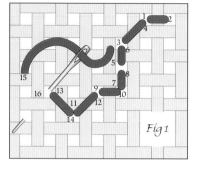

Backstitches are used to give definition to parts of a design and to outline areas of the design. To make a backstitch follow Fig 1, bringing the needle up at 1 (or at the beginning of where the stitch is to lie), and down at 2 (or at the end of where you wish this stitch to be). Then bring the needle up again at 3 (or at the beginning of where you would like the second stitch to be). Keep repeating these steps.

Cross Stitch

A cross stitch has two parts and can be worked in one of two ways. A complete stitch can be worked singly or a number of half stitches can be sewn in a line and completed on the return journey.

To make a single cross stitch over one block of Aida, bring the needle up through the fabric at the bottom right-hand side of the stitch (number 1 on Fig 2a) and cross diagonally to the top left-hand corner (2). Push the needle through the hole there and bring it up through the bottom left-hand corner (3), crossing the fabric diagonally to the top right-hand corner to finish

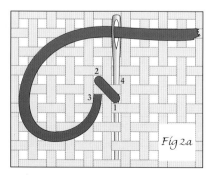

the stitch (4). To work the next stitch, push the needle up through the bottom left-hand corner of the first stitch and repeat the steps above.

To work a line of cross stitches, follow Fig 2b. Work the first part of the stitch as above and repeat along the row until the end. Complete the crosses on

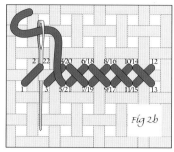

the way back. Note: always finish the cross stitch with the top stitches lying in the same diagonal direction.

French Knot

French knots have been used as eye highlights and details in some of the designs. To work a French knot follow Fig 3, bringing the needle and thread up through the fabric at the exact place where the knot is to be positioned. Wrap the thread twice around the needle

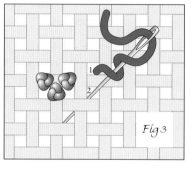

(or according to the project instructions), holding the thread firmly close to the needle, then twist the needle back through the fabric as close as possible to where it first emerged. Finally, holding the knot down carefully, pull the thread through to the back leaving the knot on the surface, securing it with one small stitch on the back.

Three-quarter Cross Stitch

A few of the larger projects use some three-quarter cross stitches to give more detail. These are shown by a triangle within a square on the chart. To work a three-quarter cross stitch, follow Fig 4 (shown on evenweave not Aida), working a half cross stitch across the diagonal, then working a quarter stitch from the corner into the centre (piercing the fabric if working on Aida).

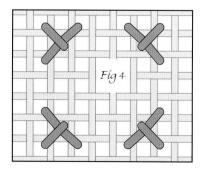

MAKING UP YOUR WORK

The embroideries in this book are very versatile and can be made up in many ways. The methods used in the book are described here but why not experiment with other ways? Metric and imperial measurements have been provided but remember to use one or the other as they are not exactly interchangeable.

APPLYING EMBROIDERY TO A BACKGROUND FABRIC

When you have completed stitching the embroidery, use the weave of the Aida fabric as a guide to trim to within ten rows of the design. Fold over the edges by seven rows – this will leave three rows showing around the design. Press these folds into place. To avoid the background fabric showing through the embroidery, cut a piece of thin cotton wadding (batting) or felt the same size as the design and insert it behind the embroidery before stitching it down. Place the design and wadding on the fabric and machine or hand stitch it in place close to the edge, using the fabric weave as a guide.

MAKING UP INTO A BAG

The poppies design on page 22 has been made up into a handy drawstring bag, ideal for trinkets. Many of the smaller designs in the book would look wonderful made up this way, including those from the Triptych Pillow and the Floral Wall Hanging. It would also be lovely to use one of the Oriental Greetings motifs and present it to someone as a special gift.

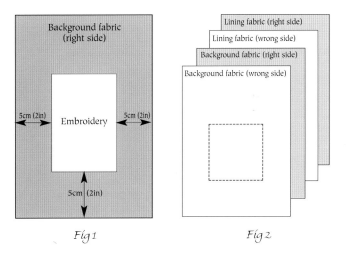

Materials
- Two pieces of background fabric 21.5 x 15cm (8½ x 6in)
- Two pieces of lining fabric 21.5 x 15cm (8½ x 6in)
- Matching sewing thread
- Decorative satin cord to tone with stitching 127cm (50in)
- Two tassels (same colour as cord)
- Two large beads and two small beads
- Stranded cotton (floss) to match cord

1 Sew the embroidery to the front of background fabric 5cm (2in) from each side and the bottom edge (Fig 1). Using matching sewing thread, stitch satin cord around the embroidery starting at the centre bottom, tacking (basting) the ends together with a few small stitches. Attach small beads at the centre bottom and the centre top using matching stranded cotton (floss).

Fig 1

Fig 2

2 Place the lining fabrics right sides together. Place the background fabrics right sides together, with the wrong side of the front of the bag on top, then pin all four layers together (Fig 2).

3 Sew a 1.25cm (½in) seam across the bottom and the two sides, up to 17cm (6¾in), leaving the seam unfinished at both sides for 3.8cm (1½in). Now stitch the side seam down from the top for 3cm (1¼in) as shown in Fig 3 overleaf.

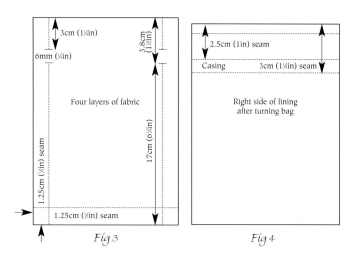

Fig 3   *Fig 4*

4 Turn the unsewn top and side seams 6mm (¼in) towards the wrong side of fabric to hide the raw edges. Turn the bag so that the right side of the lining is showing. Stitch the top edges of the background fabric and the lining together. Sew a line 2.5cm (1in) and a line 3cm (1¼in) from the top of the bag across the front and back of the bag to form a casing (Fig 4).

5 Turn the bag to the right side. Thread two 46cm (18in) pieces of satin cord through the casing with the ends extending from opposite sides (Fig 5). To finish, attach large beads and the tassels to the end of the cords.

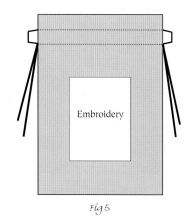

Fig 5

MAKING UP INTO A CARD

The Oriental Greetings designs on pages 77–81 have been made up as cards. Many of the small designs in the book could be displayed in the same way to make wonderful cards.

Materials

- Ready-made card mount (aperture size to fit the embroidery)
- Craft glue or double-sided adhesive tape

Simply chose a ready-made card mount that will fit your design, trimming the edges of the design if necessary. Apply a thin coat of glue or double-sided adhesive tape to the inside of the card opening. Position the embroidery, checking that the stitching is central, then press down firmly. Fold the spare flap inside, sticking in place with glue or tape, and leave to dry before closing.

DECORATING A CARD MOUNT

You can add a personal touch to the ready-made card mounts that are available. Attach beads, decorative threads or ribbon with a small amount of craft glue. Tie a cord around the inside fold and then attach a small tassel to drape over the outside. Try your hand with a calligraphy marker available at craft shops to add your own artistic strokes.

MAKING UP AS A FRAMED PICTURE

There are many examples throughout the book of designs displayed as framed pictures, such as the three Oriental Ladies. The elegance and beauty of these larger designs lend themselves particularly well to pictures.

Materials

- Picture frame (aperture size to fit the embroidery)
- Plywood or heavyweight card slightly smaller than frame
- Adhesive tape or staple gun

Iron your embroidery and trim the edges if necessary, then centre the embroidery on the piece of plywood or heavyweight card. Fold the edges of the embroidery over to the back of the wood or card and use adhesive tape to fix in place. Alternatively, use a staple gun. Insert the picture into the frame and secure in place with adhesive tape or staples.

MAKING UP INTO A PILLOW

The three designs on pages 89–92 have been made up into an unusual triptych pillow. Why not display the three flower designs on pages 54–56 in the same way? The principles of making up the triptych pillow can be applied to any pillow shape.

Materials

- Two pieces of background fabric 18 x 33cm (7 x 13in)
- Matching sewing thread
- Decorative satin cord to tone with embroideries 114cm (45in)
- Decorative braided cord to tone with embroideries 114cm (45in)
- DMC stranded cotton (floss) to match satin cord
- Three small decorative beads
- Four tassels to match braided cord
- Polyester stuffing

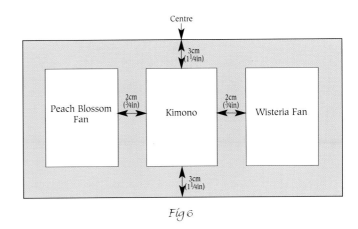

Fig 6

1 Centre and stitch the kimono embroidery to the front of one piece of background fabric as in Fig 6. Stitch the fan embroideries on either side leaving 2cm (¾in) between each design. Using matching sewing thread, sew the satin braid around each design starting at the centre bottom and tacking (basting) the ends together with small stitches. Attach a small bead at the centre bottom of each embroidery with stranded cotton (floss).

2 Place the two pieces of background fabric right sides together and sew around a 1.25cm (½in) seam, leaving a generous opening at the bottom for turning. Clip the seams to reduce bulk if necessary and turn right side out. Fill with polyester stuffing and slip stitch the opening, leaving a small opening to tuck in the braided cord at the centre bottom.

3 Using matching sewing thread, sew the braided cord around the entire pillow beginning and ending at the centre bottom. Tuck in the ends of the cord and finish the seam with a few small stitches. Attach tassels to each corner.

MAKING UP INTO A SACHET

The panda design on page 23 has been made up into an attractive scented sachet. Other designs in the book, such as the pink orchid and the peach blossom fan, would also be lovely made up this way.

Materials

- Two pieces of background fabric 16.5 x 14cm (6½ x 5½in)
- Decorative satin cord to tone with embroidery 50cm (20in)
- Decorative braided cord to tone with embroidery 60cm (24in)
- Matching sewing thread
- Decorative button
- Small amount of polyester stuffing
- Small amount of pot-pourri
- Tassel to match decorative braid

1 Sew the finished embroidery to the front of one piece of the background fabric (see page 105). Using matching sewing thread, sew the satin cord around the embroidery starting at the bottom centre. Tack (baste) the ends together with a few small stitches and then sew on the decorative button.

2 Trim the remaining satin cord to 20cm (8in), fold it in half and pin it to the right side of the front with the loop pointing towards the centre. With right sides together, sew the front to the back with a 1.25cm (½in) seam all around, leaving a 9cm (3½in) opening at centre bottom for turning. Trim the corners and seams to reduce bulk if necessary.

3 Turn the sachet right side out and stuff with polyester filling and pot-pourri. Sew up the bottom opening leaving a 2.5cm (1in) gap at centre bottom. Sew the braided cord around the edges of the sachet, tucking the ends into the opening at the bottom, finishing off with a few small stitches. Attach the tassel at centre bottom as a finishing touch.

MAKING UP A WALL HANGING

The three flower designs on pages 54–56 are made up into a beautiful wall hanging. Other designs from this book could be displayed in the same way: possible arrangements include the Prosperity greeting card on page 79 or the Morning Glory motif on page 54, centred between the two fan embroideries from the pillow. Alternatively, choose your three favourites from the smaller designs and create your own unique combination.

Materials

- Two pieces of background fabric 52 x 19cm (20½ x 7½in)
- One piece of iron-on interfacing 52 x 19cm (20½ x 7½in)
- Matching sewing thread
- Decorative satin cord to tone with embroidery 152cm (60in)
- Decorative braided cord to tone with embroidery 183cm (72in)
- Six small and two large decorative beads
- Five tassels to match braid
- Stranded cotton (floss) to tone with beads
- Two 6mm (¼in) diameter dowels painted gold, each 21cm (8¼in) long

1 Iron the interfacing to the wrong side of one piece of the background fabric. With reference to Fig 7, centre and sew the orchid embroidery to the right side of this piece. Leaving 3cm (1¼in) between the embroideries, sew on the morning glory and iris above and below the orchid. Using matching sewing thread, stitch the decorative satin cord around each embroidery, tacking (basting) the ends at the centre bottom with a few small stitches. Attach a small decorative bead at the bottom of each embroidery with stranded cotton (floss).

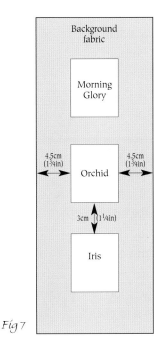

Fig 7

2 Place the background fabric pieces right sides together and pin. Then, using a 1.25cm (½in) seam, stitch the top and bottom seams leaving a 7.5cm (3in) opening at the bottom for turning. Sew the side seams leaving a 2.5cm (1in) opening for the casing at the top and bottom of the side seams. Trim the corners and seam allowance to reduce bulk and turn the hanging to the right side. Stitch the remaining bottom edge closed.

3 Top stitch a line 2.5cm (1in) from the top and bottom edges to form a casing. Using matching sewing thread, sew the satin cord along this stitched line, turning the ends to the back. Attach the braided cord along the side, around the casing and up the back for 5cm (2in), tucking in the ends at the back. Attach the decorative beads and the centre tassel to the bottom of the iris design (see

photograph, above). Attach tassels at each corner where the braided cord meets the satin cord.

4 Insert the dowels in the casings. For hanging, tie the remaining braided cord on the dowels in a knot or bow and finish the ends with a large bead to prevent fraying.

DESIGN WORKS CRAFTS

Founded in 1987 by Susan Goldsmith-Knopp and partner/husband Daniel Knopp, Design Works Crafts Inc. has been a leader in the needlework kit industry for the past thirteen years. The vision of 'what people want' has been the driving factor behind the success of the company. As a manufacturer of needlework kits, Susan recognizes the huge time investment that a stitcher makes in creating an embroidery. Therefore, she feels that each design must have some meaning or value beyond being 'just pretty'.

This meaningful vision was clear on recent trips to the Orient where Susan became interested in Oriental textures, symbolism and the principles of Feng Shui. Discussions with long-time collaborator Joan Elliott were the catalyst for the Design Works Feng Shui line of needlework kits. There are more than twenty-four kits available and each include pre-sorted threads, fine-quality fabrics, needles and easy-to-follow instructions. With an eye towards the consumer without the time to buy individual components, Design Works strives to assemble a fine-quality kit for a reasonable price. We hope that you will visit the shops in your area that carry our line, or e-mail us at design_works@msn.com for further information.

ACKNOWLEDGEMENTS

I would like to express my deep appreciation to everyone that helped make this book possible. Heartfelt thanks to the many embroiderers, charters and staff at Design Works Crafts whose time and talents help carry my designs to their final beauty; special thanks to Donna Richardson for her exquisite photography and unerring attention to detail, and to Susan and Danny Knopp for their collaboration, enthusiasm and friendship. Love and thank you to my dear friend Janet Healy for her advice, proof-reading and support, and to my family for their love, especially to Earl for being in my life.

Finally, special appreciation to Cheryl Brown and the folks at David and Charles for their interest in my work and to all the designers and photographers there that helped make this project a reality. To Lin Clements, my editor, thank you for your guidance and knowledge.

JOAN ELLIOTT, 2001

Special thanks also to the following businesses for their wonderful resources:

Yoko Trading
22 Bick Road,
Fleetwood, PA 19522, USA
Tel: 610 987 9720
Website: www.yokodana.com
For Japanese vintage kimonos and antiques.

The Art of Japan
PO Box 507
Mountain View, CA 94042, USA
Tel: 650 964 4464
E-mail: rwaldman@theartofjapan.com
Website: www.pointsinspace.com
A source for exquisite ukiyo-e Japanese woodblock prints.

Mita Arts Company Ltd.
Ivy Building, 4th Floor,
1–10 Jinbocho, Kanda, Chiyoda-Ku,
Tokyo 101, Japan
Tel: (03) 3294-4554
Website: www.mita-arts.com
Japanese prints from the eighteenth to twentieth centuries.

The Gingko Leaf
788A Union Street,
Brooklyn, NY 11215, USA
Tel: 718 399 9876
E-mail: ginko21@aol.com
A source of Japanese items for the body, home and garden.

Prints Charming
54 7th Avenue, Brooklyn, NY 11217, USA
Tel: 718 230 8118
A source for one-of-a-kind antique prints in all genres.

SUPPLIERS

Charles Craft, Inc.
PO Box 1049, Laurenburg, NC 28353, USA
Tel: 910 844 3521
E-mail: ccraft@carolina.net
Website: www.charlescraft.com
For pre-finished fingertip towels, other pre-finished items for the home and baby, and fabrics for cross stitch. (Coats Crafts UK supply some Charles Craft products in the UK.)

Coats Crafts UK
PO Box 22, Lingfield Estate, McMullen Road, Darlington, Co. Durham DL1 1YQ, UK
Tel: 01325 365457 (for a list of stockists)
For Anchor stranded cotton (floss) and other embroidery supplies. Coats also supply some Charles Craft products.

Design Works Crafts Inc.
170 Wilbur Place, Bohemia, New York 11716, USA
Tel: 631 244 5749   Fax: 631 244 6138
E-mail: design_works@msn.com
For cross stitch kits (featuring Joan Elliott designs) and card mounts outside the UK.)

DMC Creative World Ltd.
Pullman Road, Wigston, Leicestershire LE18 2DY, UK
Tel: 0116 281 1040   Fax: 0116 281 3592
Website: www.dmc/cw.com
For stranded cotton (floss) and other embroidery supplies.

Framecraft Miniatures Ltd.
372–376 Summer Lane, Hockley, Birmingham B19 3QA, UK
Tel: 0121 212 0551   Fax: 0121 212 0552

Website: www.framecraft.com
For wooden trinket bowls and boxes, notebook covers, pincushions, towels and many other pre-finished items with cross stitch inserts.

M & J Buttons
1000 Sixth Avenue, New York, NY 10018, USA
Tel: 212 391 6200
Website: www.mjtrim.com
For satin cord, braided cord, ribbons, buttons and beads.

Madeira Threads (UK) Ltd.
PO Box 6, Thirsk, North Yorkshire YO7 3YX, UK
Tel: 01845 524880
E-mail: info@madeira.co.uk
Website: www.madeira.co.uk
For stranded cotton (floss) and other embroidery supplies.

Solo
4A Standard Way Industrial Estate, North Allerton, North Yorkshire DL6 2XE, UK
Tel: 01609 779919   Fax: 01609 760309
Website: www.solocrafts.com
For Design Works cross stitch kits (including Joan Elliott designs) and card mounts.

Zweigart/ Joan Toggit Ltd.
262 Old Brunswick Road, Suite E,
Picataway, NJ 08854-3756, USA
Tel: 732 562 8888
E-mail: info@ zweigart.com
Website: www.zweigart.com
For pre-finished table linens and other embroidery fabrics.

INDEX